MARVEL

BLACK PANTHER

THE OFFICIAL

WAKANDA COOKBOOK

MARVEL

BLACK PANTHER

THE OFFICIAL

WAKANDA COOKBOOK

NYANYIKA BANDA

INSIGHT EDITIONS

San Rafael • Los Angeles • London

CONTENTS

FOREWORD

I grew up reading comic books. But except for a few characters here and there, none of them really spoke to me . . . or even really looked like me.

But then I discovered T'Challa, created in 1966 by Stan Lee and Jack Kirby, and he resonated with my young self. He was noble, self-effacing, smart, strong, and regal—all things that I wished that I could be.

Like me—the bespectacled, lanky, uncoordinated son of an English teacher and a science teacher who really wanted to be cool—T'Challa wasn't "down" and "with it" like other Blaxploitation characters offered up: He didn't talk in slang or wear a pimp suit or discotheque-style clothing.

He was what my young, impressionable soul really wanted to be: a classically educated genius who happened to be royalty; a prince who was wealthy, religious, and handsome—and, by the way, he was a world-renowned fighter who led the most technologically advanced nation on the planet.

And best of all, he was unashamedly Black. It even was in his name.

The Black Panther has stalked our collective consciousness for decades, finding honored places in our comic book collections, our bookshelves, our televisions, our radios, and most recently, our movie screens. So, it should come as no surprise that the world of Wakanda will now be represented in the most important place in our homes, the one place where we all come together: our kitchens!

With *Marvel Comics' Black Panther: The Official Wakanda Cookbook*, the world of T'Challa, son of T'Chaka, the one true Black Panther, breaks into another entirely new realm: the world of culinary arts.

As a Southerner (Mississippi born and bred!), I wholeheartedly approve this new Wakandan venture as a way for more of us to connect with our ancestral roots in the kitchens of ancient Africa. Many of the foods I grew up on—okra, collard greens, black-eyed peas, beef and chicken stew, and cornbread—all have their roots or their style of cooking in African tradition, brought to the United States by our ancestors.

Like many of you, I sat at my grandmothers' knees and listened to their tales as they fried, baked, and stewed foods for their families, and marveled at the stories of days gone by and the people they lost and gained. I knew even back then I wanted to be a storyteller like them, and I absorbed as much as I could as the pots bubbled, the grease sizzled, and the bread and cakes rose in the oven.

The African proverb says: "Words are sweet, but they never take the place of food." In my home, and in homes around the world, the two walk hand-in-hand. It's in the kitchen where mothers and fathers pass down family recipes and family lore, telling stories of days gone by and people we loved and remember. It's in the kitchen where friends gather and guests linger around the savory smells of dishes lovingly prepared by hands both old and young.

It's in the kitchen and around food that family and friends get to know each other a little better and bonds are created. What better place for new legends to grow, as we all learn the secrets of Wakandan cuisine and how to eat like a king?

Now I can't wait to pull out my cast-iron skillet or my wife's old, battered gumbo pot and learn how to make Smoked Chambo, or sample Glazed Roadrunner Wings or some of the other fabulous Wakandan fare offered through this book. Who knows, maybe some of these dishes will become a new tradition in my family, and I'll be able to pass them down to my descendants!

I have been lucky enough to be able to tell stories of the Black Panther and Wakanda, writing the *Black Panther: Who Is The Black Panther?* novel in 2017, guest-starring in the award-winning

Black Panther: Who Is the Black Panther? audiobook in 2010, and editing (and writing in!) the new *Black Panther: Tales of Wakanda* anthology in 2021.

This experience has allowed me to speak with fans of T'Challa and the characters in the world of Wakanda from around the world, from China to Kazakhstan to Europe and all around the United States. It has been one of my greatest pleasures in life just to be able to sit down and talk with other creatives and fans about Wakanda, its people, its traditions, its kings and queens, and its future as we help craft this modern-day mythology.

And now perhaps, someday, we can all get together around a meal of fine Wakandan fare and offer up a toast to the king and his people, who have changed us all so much. Perhaps someday we'll all be in the same kitchen, and together we will spark the imagination of future girls and boys, as we sit and serve meals designed to sate our Wakanda souls.

—JESSE J. HOLLAND

INTRODUCTION

The food of Wakanda is like nowhere else and simultaneously everywhere one could travel in the universe, because Wakanda lives in the heart of everyone. I was destined to be a culinarian out of the womb. My iya agba (grandmother), iya (mother), and Anti (Aunt) Bahiya created a legacy through growing and making food, and I dedicate this first Wakanda Cookbook to these powerful women.

We are raised as Wakandans to practice a healthy lifestyle, eating lots of fresh fruits like mangoes and bananas, fish from the Nyanza (Lake Victoria), and groundnuts that can be farmed. Growing our own vegetables is a part of customary life here. If you have land, you farm it. Most of us have chimanga (corn) in our yards that we use for drying and turning into cornmeal. We also love eating it fresh, and giving ears out as gifts.

My grandmother was a farmer along with my grandfather. During World War II, when King Azzuri was fighting the Nazi invasion, my grandparents supplied the Royal Palace with goods from their farm. They grew lemon and lime trees, farmed groundnuts such as peanuts, and grew maize and hearty greens like kale and collards. They also raised goats, ox, and chickens. It was on this farm that my mother and Anti Bahiya grew up and where I was born.

Both my mother and anti attended school in their village and would work on the farm before and after. It was when they were young that my grandfather was killed during a tribal conflict, leaving my grandmother to farm on her own. This was when my mother and Anti Bahiya decided to start a business together. Anti Bahiya was seventeen and my mother fifteen. They were going to open a food stand at the Birnin Zana Market in the Golden City. They began with one dish, making a chicken curry stew and selling meals of chicken, nsima, and kabichi, a curried cabbage salad. My mother was not an inventive cook, but my anti thought like a chef. The more often they visited the market, the more elaborate her ideas for meals became. Their tiny street food business gained notoriety near and far.

Word spread of the young girls with the delicious food and soon they were serving not only daytime workers but also staff of the Royal Palace. Their food was making it into the mouths of King T'Chaka and his wife N'Yami. On their days off, members of the Dora Milaje would stop by for their newest creations. My Anti Bahiya was creating recipes like zoumba moa, a dehydrated mushroom snack, and sweet potato baked with oats and pecans found at the market that the Dora Milaje could take with them during training.

After months of selling meals at the market, my mother fell in love with one of their regulars. My father was an engineer who worked for the Wakandan Army and lived in the Golden City. She continued attending school and working with her sister. She dreamed of getting married and having a daughter that she could pass on the family business to. Anti Bahiya's future would become very different.

The Dora Milaje fell in love with my anti's snacks. They could see she was a very hard worker and her intelligence shone through her creative recipes, as did her quick thinking while working the food stand, all qualities the Dora Milaje look for in a new recruit. One day, they came to her with an offer. They said they had spoken with the elders of her tribe and that she had been chosen to join them and train at Upanga. At seventeen, my anti was initiated as a Dora Milaje. My mother later got married and my father moved to the family land to help her farm.

My mother continued to make and sell food at the Birnin Zana Market and when I was born, she would bring me as a baby along with her. As soon as I could hold a knife, I was slicing cabbage for slaw. At home, I would sit with her as she would prepare the meals for the next day. Once I was old enough to go to school, in the mornings I would go with my father to feed the chickens. And in the afternoons, I would meet my mother at the market.

I would receive letters from Anti Bahiya often. She would tell me about her adventures, traveling the world defending Wakanda and protecting King T'Chaka and young T'Challa. She always included the new foods she was discovering and explaining to me, "Wakanda is everywhere!" She promised that someday I would see the world outside of Wakanda, too.

One day, her promise came true. I was eighteen and had been working the farm and the market with my mother. That day we had lamb kebabs and samosas and were running out fast. A woman came up and ordered one of each. She came back shortly after, exclaiming how it was the best samosa she had ever had. I blushed and thanked her. She then revealed that she worked for the N'Charu Silema and that she knew my Anti Bahiya. My heart began to race, I had never encountered anyone from King T'Challa's inner circle. She explained that the king and his sister were in need of a new private chef to join the palace staff and that I was being offered the job. I was told to go home and pack my things, and that I would be starting the next day.

This was the best day of my life, and that night we celebrated with a feast of braised oxtail, smoked fish, nsima, and kale. The next morning, I said goodbye to my mother and father and headed to the Wakandan School for Alternative Studies. It was there that I was taught how to incorporate technology into my cooking. Wakandans don't use fossil fuels to cook traditionally. We try to use eco-friendly culinary techniques. At the Wakandan School for Alternative Studies we used dehydration and temperature-controlled machines to cook rather than wood or coal. It was all new to me and I loved it! Once I graduated I took up residency at the Royal Palace. King T'Challa began to request me for special diplomatic trips. I have catered many dinners at the Wakanda Embassy in New York City.

It was through my travels that I saw what Anti Bahiya was saying in all her letters. There were signs of Wakanda everywhere. I had always thought that mangoes and pineapples were a Wakandan secret, but I saw them at markets on the streets of New York. Sometimes, I could find goat at the Carribean markets, but there was also lamb, which I found to be a good substitute. I also saw the spices of my homeland in African grocery stores that carried dried crayfish. Sweet potatoes, kale, and tomatoes were abundant. I began to create dishes that incorporated all that I was seeing and all that I had learned from the braised chicken at the market to the sous vide yams I saw at restaurants in the city.

This cookbook is a tribute to the warm heart that lives deep within the continent of Africa and how, through its food, that love has spread across the world.

Ndi Chikondi

Executive Chef, Royal Palace of Wakanda

INGREDIENTS GUIDE

BIRD'S EYE CHILI also known as a Thai chile, also grows throughout Africa. It acquires the nickname *bird's eye* when it is dried because the pepper looks like a bird's beak.

CAROB, sometimes referred to as the locust bean, is a sweet pod that grows in tropical climates. The pods have a pulp that is often dried, roasted, and ground and used in baking.

CASSAVA is more commonly known in the Western world as yuca. It is a tuber with a rough outer brown skin and a white flesh. Cassava contains various toxins and should always be cooked before eaten.

CASSAVA FLOUR is a flour that incorporates the whole root of the cassava tuber. Tapioca flour can be substituted for cassava flour in recipes, however the fiber content is slightly less. It can also be used as a replacement for cornstarch.

CHAMBO, also known as tilapia, is a low fat, sweet, white-fleshed fresh water fish that is a staple all across Africa. It is enjoyed smoked, roasted, and fried.

CRAWFISH are crustaceans that in many regions of Africa are commonly dried and then used in soups and sauces. Crawfish is a common name that refers to any type of dried shrimp whether from coastal or fresh lake fishermen. The shrimps are washed in a salted water solution and then sun dried for preservation.

CURRY LEAVES have traveled the world through the Indian spice trade. In cooking, the leaf adds a strong curry aroma to dishes. The fresh leaves should be stored in a sealed container and refrigerated.

CURRY POWDER is actually a spice blend of as many as twenty spices including turmeric, cloves, cinnamon, and cumin.

HARISSA is commonly seen as a paste throughout North Africa. In this cookbook it is a dry spice rub that can be made into a paste by adding a little oil.

HIBISCUS is natively grown in tropical climates, such as Africa, Asia, Latin America, and the Caribbean. The petals are often dried and then steeped to make teas and syrups. Traditionally, hibiscus is used as a healing plant. It is known as bissap in West Africa and in the Caribbean; drinks made with the petals are known as sorrel.

LAMB/GOAT MEAT: The difference between goat meat and lamb meat is the fat content. Goats are more commonly found in Africa and lamb is more commonly found in Western countries. Both are best when slow cooked by braising, roasting, or smoking.

NSIMA traditionally is a porridge made with cassava flour or cornmeal. Many cultures across Africa have variations of this type of staple side dish. It is often formed into a patty and then dipped by hand into stews and sauces or used with hands and fingers as a utensil to indulge in braised meat or fish.

OKRA is garnered in some regions of Africa for its thickening capabilities and is included in most soup and stew recipes. It is most popularly known in Western countries as a staple in gumbo.

OXTAIL generally is prepared by slow cooking until the meat is tender and falls off the bone. Common substitutions are beef shank or lamb shank.

PEANUT OIL is a mild, clear pressed oil from peanuts and is commonly used in cooking across Africa.

PEANUTS in Africa are often referred to as groundnuts and are prepared and served in various ways from boiled to roasted. Peanuts traveled the world through enslaved Africans during the Transatlantic Slave Trade.

PILI PILI SAUCE is a traditional African hot sauce made with African bird's eye chiles.

PLANTAINS are also referred to as cooking bananas. They are often purchased unripe or green and roasted or fried. Ripe plantains can be mashed and used as thickeners in soups and stews, or sliced and fried.

POMEGRANATE SYRUP is the reduction of pomegranate juice that is thick and tart. It can be found in bottles or made by slow cooking pomegranate juice until it has reduced by half.

RAS EL HANOUT is a spice blend commonly found in Africa. It can include up to fifty ingredients but often has cardamom, cinnamon, ginger, and nutmeg.

SWEET POTATOES are also known as yams or tubers. Yellow or orange tubers are a native staple to Africans across the continent; they grow easily all year round and store for a long period of time. They are known to have traveled to the United States and Caribbean via the Transatlantic Slave Trade.

TAMARIND is the fruit pod of a tree that is native to northern Africa. The pod is filled with a pulp that is blanched and strained. Tamarind can be found in various forms such as canned paste and jars of concentrate.

DIETARY CONSIDERATIONS

If you have particular dietary needs, consult the chart below to quickly find recipes that fit.

RECIPE	VEGETARIAN	VEGAN	NONDAIRY	GLUTEN-FREE
SPICES, SAUCES, AND CONDIMENTS				
Cardamom Granita	V	V+	ND	GF
Carrot Ginger Dressing			ND	GF
Chinananzi Salsa	V	V+	ND	GF
Curried Aioli			ND	GF
Ginger Granita	V	V+	ND	GF
Harissa Spice Mix	V	V+	ND	GF
Kale Pesto	V	V+	ND	GF
Mango Gel	V	V+	ND	GF
Mango Ginger Sauce	V	V+	ND	GF
Msuzi Matimati			ND	GF
Muhammara	V		ND	GF
Peyala Mousse			ND	GF
Pili Pili Sauce	V	V+	ND	GF
Spiced Ketchup			ND	GF
MARKET FOOD				
Beef Samosas			ND	
Boiled Mtedza	V			GF
Cassava Fries		V+	ND	GF
Chicken Meatballs			ND	GF
Glazed Road Runner Wings			ND	GF
Grilled Chimanga with Curried Aioli	V		ND	GF
Harissa Spiced Popcorn	V			GF
Lamb Kebabs			ND	GF
Okra Fritters	V			
Plantain Chips	V	V+	ND	GF
Smoked Chambo			ND	GF
Vegetable Samosas	V		ND	
Zouma Bowa			ND	

Recipe	Vegetarian	Vegan	Nondairy	Gluten-free
Breakfast				
Akara	V	V+	ND	GF
Baked Sweet Potato and Kale Eggs			ND	GF
Braised Beans	V	V+	ND	GF
Carob Energy Balls			ND	GF
Harissa Eggs and Shaved Cucumbers			ND	GF
Rice Porridge			ND	GF
Sweet Potato Granola			ND	GF
Soups and Salads				
Chilled Watermelon Soup	V	V+	ND	
Chimanga and Black Eyed-Peas	V	V+	ND	GF
Citrus and Avocado Salad			ND	GF
Kabichi				GF
Mango and Pineapple Salad	V	V+	ND	GF
Okra and Beef Soup			ND	GF
Pumpkin and Cassava Leaf Soup	V	V+	ND	GF
Tomato and Herb Salad	V	V+	ND	GF
Vegetables and Sides				
Braised Kale and Tomatoes	V			GF
Charred Okuru	V	V+	ND	GF
Dried Fruits and Rice	V	V+	ND	GF
Lavash	V	V+	ND	
Nsima	V	V+	ND	
Roasted Plantains	V	V+	ND	GF
Sous Vide Eggplant and Herbs	V	V+		GF
Sous Vide Tubers	V	V+		GF

Recipe	Vegetarian	Vegan	Nondairy	Gluten-free
MAIN DISHES				
Blackened Tilapia			ND	GF
Braised Lamb Stew			ND	GF
Sweet and Spicy Oxtail with Cassava Dumplings			ND	GF
Cassava Ravioli				GF
Roasted Lake Trout			ND	GF
Savory Plantain Custard				GF
Stuffed Pumpkin with Dried Fruits and Rice	V	V+	ND	GF
Village-Style Curried Chicken			ND	GF
DESSERTS				
Basbousa				GF
Doughnuts and Foamed Cocoa				
Mango Sorbet with Ginger Granita	V	V+	ND	GF
Microwaved Banana and Walnut Cake				
Pawpaw Sorbet with Ginger Granita	V	V+	ND	GF
Whipped Sweet Potato and Candied Cinnamon				
DRINKS				
Avocado Smoothie			ND	GF
Bissap Spritz			ND	GF
Cocoa Iced Coffee				GF
Coconut Mango Smoothie	V	V+	ND	GF
Ginger Tonic	V	V+	ND	GF
Ginger Turmeric Lemonade	V	V+	ND	GF
Orange Carrot Juice	V	V+	ND	GF
Orange Smash			ND	GF
Tamarind Cola			ND	GF

Spices, Sauces, and Condiments

MUHAMMARA

While I was still an apprentice at the Royal Palace, my mentor, Chef Eli, explained to me that this was one of Queen Nanali's (the current king's grandmother) favorite dishes. There is a bakery in the Birnin Azzaria Market that was run by two sisters, Kylee and Ayla. They baked the artisan loaves and lavash that Queen Nanali preferred. Chef Eli would place orders once a week with the sisters. She would serve the dip with slices of cucumber and carrots and loaves of fresh-baked lavash.

DIFFICULTY: Easy • **PREP TIME:** 15 minutes • **COOK TIME:** 1 hour
YIELD: 2 cups • **DIETARY NOTES:** Gluten-free, nondairy, vegetarian

2 large red bell peppers

5 garlic cloves, peeled

1 teaspoon crushed red pepper

2 tablespoons olive oil

1 cup toasted walnuts

¼ cup lemon juice

2 tablespoons pomegranate syrup (see note)

Salt and pepper

TOOLS:

Food processor

 NOTE: If pomegranate syrup is unavailable, balsamic glaze is a good substitute.

1. Preheat the oven to 425 degrees Fahrenheit.

2. In a medium mixing bowl, toss the red bell peppers, garlic, crushed red pepper, olive oil, and a pinch of salt and pepper.

3. Place the coated red bell peppers on a baking tray lined with parchment paper. Bake until the skin of the peppers is lightly charred and bubbling, about 45 minutes.

4. Place all the contents back in the mixing bowl and cover with plastic wrap. Let sit for 15 minutes.

5. Peel the skin and seeds from the peppers.

6. In a food processor, combine the walnuts and lemon juice with the roasted peppers, garlic, and excess oil from the pan. Process until smooth.

7. Pour into a serving dish and drizzle the pomegranate syrup on top. This dip can be made ahead of time and refrigerated in an airtight container for up to 1 week.

CHINANANZI SALSA

Chinananzi, also known as pineapple, is known as the "exquisite fruit" and symbolizes hospitality. This salsa is easy to make and can be an accompaniment to many dishes and snacks like smoked plantain chips or with lamb kebabs or smoked fish.

DIFFICULTY: Easy • **PREP TIME:** 45 minutes • **COOK TIME:** 30 minutes
YIELD: 4 cups • **DIETARY NOTES:** Gluten-free, nondairy, nut-free, vegan

½ pineapple, small diced (about 2½ cups)

½ medium red onion, small diced

½ cup red wine vinegar

2 teaspoons cane sugar

2 teaspoons ground cumin

1 lime, zested and juiced

1 jalapeño, small diced (optional)

Salt and pepper

1. To dice the pineapple, first cut the top and end off. Then cut the pineapple in half. Putting half of the pineapple aside, stand the pineapple flesh side down on the cutting board, and using a serrated knife, peel the skin with the knife from top to bottom rotating after each cut. Next slice the pineapple into ¼-inch rounds. Stack the rounds and cut them lengthwise into ¼-inch slices. Rotate and repeat crosswise to make a small dice.

2. Dice the onion. Use a fine grater or microplane to zest the lime before squeezing out the juice.

3. In a large mixing bowl, combine pineapple, onion, vinegar, sugar, cumin, lime zest, lime juice, and jalapeño.

4. Mix with a large spoon or spatula. Salt and pepper to taste.

5. Cover and refrigerate for at least 30 minutes or overnight.

MANGO GINGER SAUCE

I have yet to meet a Wakandan who does not love mangoes. We plant their trees everywhere so that no one has to pay for them. One day, while preparing breakfast at the Royal Palace, I glanced out the window and saw one of the gardeners rapidly eating his way through a handful and it made me smile, recalling my family farm and the mangoes we grew. They are fruits given to us by the land. Not only do humans snack on mangoes, but the farm animals do as well.

DIFFICULTY: Easy • **PREP TIME:** 10 minutes • **COOK TIME:** 5 minutes
YIELD: 1 cup • **DIETARY NOTES:** Gluten-free, nondairy, nut-free, vegan

2 tablespoons cornstarch

1 cup mango juice

3 garlic cloves, minced

1 tablespoon minced fresh ginger

2 teaspoons tomato paste

2 pinches crushed red pepper (optional)

Salt and pepper

1. In a small saucepan, whisk cornstarch and mango juice until the cornstarch is completely dissolved.

2. Add garlic and ginger. Cook over medium-high heat, whisking occasionally for 2 minutes. The sauce will start to turn translucent.

3. Add tomato paste and crushed red pepper. Continue to cook for another 3 minutes, whisking occasionally. The sauce should be thick and shiny.

4. Remove from heat. Salt and pepper to taste.

CURRIED AIOLI

Many of the high-end restaurants in New York City that I visited served a version of aioli that would be spread on the bread of sandwiches or used as a sauce to dip fried potatotes in. An aioli is just an emulsion of eggs and oil and in Wakanda, it is customary to keep chickens for eggs, especially outside the larger cities, so we have an abundance of eggs. I began to test how an aioli could be incorporated into our foods and added yellow curry powder to a traditional aioli. It is delicious for dipping cassava chips or spreading on chimanga.

DIFFICULTY: Easy • **PREP TIME:** 10 minutes • **YIELD:** 1 cup
DIETARY NOTES: Gluten-free, nondairy, nut-free

2 egg yolks

1 tablespoon Dijon mustard

4 garlic cloves

¼ cup plus 1 teaspoon lemon juice

2 cups vegetable oil

3 teaspoons yellow curry powder

1 teaspoon red wine vinegar

Salt and pepper

TOOLS:

Food processor

1. Combine egg yolks, Dijon, garlic, and ¼ cup of lemon juice in the food processor. Blend until garlic is chopped.

2. Very slowly, about a tablespoon at a time, drizzle the oil into the mixture while the food processor is on. The yolks and oil will form an emulsion. It should look creamy, thick, and smooth.

3. Once all the oil is incorporated, transfer to a medium mixing bowl.

4. Add curry powder, red wine vinegar, and 1 teaspoon of lemon juice. Mix together with a spatula.

5. Salt and pepper to taste. This can be stored, covered, in the refrigerator for up to 4 days.

Carrot Ginger Dressing

This is our "house dressing" at the Royal Palace and is often used for vegetables and fruits and as a marinade for fish.

DIFFICULTY: Easy • **PREP TIME:** 5 minutes
YIELD: 2 cups • **DIETARY NOTES:** Gluten-free, nondairy, nut-free

½ cup carrot juice

½ cup cider vinegar

1 bird's eye chile (or small serrano pepper)

One 2-inch piece fresh ginger, peeled and cut into chunks

4 garlic cloves

2 cups olive oil

Salt and pepper

TOOLS:

Blender

1. Combine carrot juice, vinegar, chile, ginger, and garlic in a blender until incorporated.

2. Slowly add the olive oil to form an emulsion. Salt and pepper to taste.

3. Store refrigerated for up to 1 week.

SPICED KETCHUP

This recipe for ketchup has evolved over the years. During Alkebulan's Elder Age of Ancient Wakanda, a pickled fish condiment was commonly used in cooking. They would combine the condiment with anything from native Wakandan mushrooms to tomatoes. Eventually the recipe evolved to include sugar and vinegar. This recipe uses tomatoes, and the fish sauce is optional.

DIFFICULTY: Easy • **PREP TIME:** 10 minutes • **COOK TIME:** 45 minutes
YIELD: 3 cups • **DIETARY NOTES:** Gluten-free, nondairy, nut-free

One 28-ounce can tomato purée

1 medium yellow onion, peeled and quartered

3 garlic cloves

1 bird's eye chile (or ½ serrano pepper)

½ teaspoon cayenne pepper

1 teaspoon celery salt

1 teaspoon ground mustard

1 teaspoon Chinese five-spice powder

1 teaspoon ground ginger

1 teaspoon ground black pepper

2 tablespoons brown sugar

½ cup cider vinegar

¼ cup fish sauce (optional)

Salt

TOOLS:

Food processor or blender

1. In the food processor combine tomatoes, onion, garlic, and chile. Blend until smooth.

2. Transfer to a medium saucepan and add cayenne, celery salt, ground mustard, Chinese five-spice, ground ginger, black pepper, brown sugar, vinegar, and fish sauce.

3. Simmer, covered, over medium heat for 45 minutes, stirring occasionally. Salt to taste.

4. Cool down and blend once again to make it smooth.

5. Store refrigerated for up to 2 weeks.

KALE PESTO

In Wakanda, we hull our own pumpkin seeds with special equipment that is made for the home. Fortunately, around the world, roasted pumpkin seeds, also known as pepitas, can be purchased in the store. For some, the fresh kale can be bitter, which is why I added a little lemon juice and nutritional yeast in this recipe. It can be eaten as a dip, spread on toast, or used as a sauce with pasta.

DIFFICULTY: Easy • **PREP TIME:** 15 minutes
YIELD: 1½ cups • **DIETARY NOTES:** Gluten-free nondairy, nut-free, vegan

3 garlic cloves

½ cup roasted pumpkin seeds (pepitas)

½ cup lemon juice

½ cup olive oil

2 bunches kale (about 6 cups)

½ cup nutritional yeast

Salt and pepper

TOOLS:

Food processor

1. To prepare the kale, use your hands to tear the leaves from the stems. Place the leaves in a bowl and discard the stems.

2. In a food processor, combine garlic, pumpkin seeds, and lemon juice until a paste is formed.

3. Add olive oil.

4. While running the food processor, add the kale leaves. Regularly stop and check that the edges are mixed in.

5. Once fully incorporated, transfer to a medium-sized mixing bowl.

6. Add nutritional yeast. Salt and pepper to taste. Store the pesto, covered, in the refrigerator for up to 5 days.

Harissa Spice Mix

Many recipes for harissa around the world are in the form of a paste. In Wakanda, we use our technology to quickly and easily dehydrate so many of our spices for storage and transportation and to efficiently utilize all crops. I keep this spice mix in my cupboard to add a kick to grilled corn. Olive oil can be added to create a paste for marinating meats.

DIFFICULTY: Easy • **PREP TIME:** 10 minutes
YIELD: 1½ cups • **DIETARY NOTES:** Gluten-free, nondairy, vegan

1 tablespoon chili powder

1 tablespoon smoked paprika

1 tablespoon ground cumin

1 tablespoon ground caraway

1 tablespoon ground fennel

1 tablespoon garlic powder

1 tablespoon ground coriander

1 tablespoon ground black pepper

1 tablespoon ground cinnamon

1 tablespoon ground ginger

1 tablespoon dried mint

1 tablespoon dried parsley

1. Combine all ingredients. Store in an airtight container in a cool, dry place for up to 6 months.

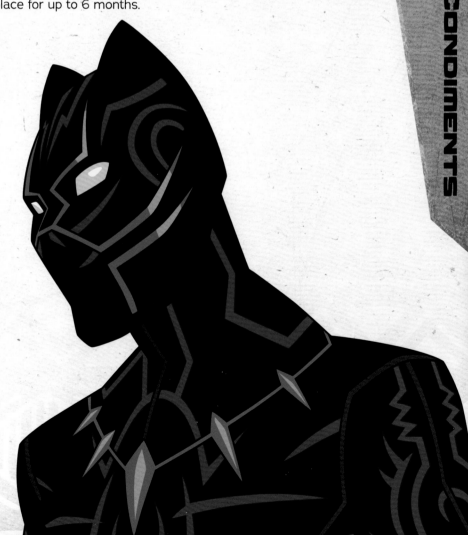

MSUZI MATIMATI

The most common way that meats are served in a Wakandan home is with a sauce. I enjoy using my fingers to form perfect bites of fish and nsima with this warm tomato sauce.

DIFFICULTY: Easy • **PREP TIME:** 10 minutes • **COOK TIME:** 20 minutes
YIELD: 1½ cups, 4 to 6 servings • **DIETARY NOTES:** Gluten-free, Nondairy

5 medium vine tomatoes

1 tablespoon peanut oil

1 small yellow onion, sliced

4 garlic cloves, minced

2 teaspoons salt

1 teaspoon ground cumin

1 teaspoon ground cardamom

1 teaspoon ground coriander

1 teaspoon ground ginger

1 teaspoon light brown sugar

1 teaspoon ground black pepper

¼ cup fresh lemon juice

¼ cup white distilled vinegar

½ cup water

1 cup fresh micro cilantro (or chopped cilantro leaves)

1. Cut ends of the tomatoes off. Using a cheese grater, grate the tomatoes into a medium mixing bowl. Discard the skins and set the bowl aside.

2. In a large skillet, warm oil over medium-high heat.

3. Add onion and garlic, stirring occasionally for 3 minutes, or until onions are slightly transparent.

4. Pour in grated tomatoes, add salt, and mix in.

5. Add cumin, cardamom, coriander, ginger, brown sugar, and pepper and stir for 1 minute.

6. Add lemon juice, vinegar, and water. Mix together and let simmer for 20 minutes.

7. Take off heat and stir in fresh cilantro.

8. Serve immediately with fish and rice or cool and store refrigerated for up to 1 week. Warm on medium heat on the stovetop or microwave to reheat.

PEYALA MOUSSE

It is important to use avocados that are ripe and soft to the touch for this recipe. There are a handful of countries in Africa that are known for their exportation of avocados. Wakanda has an ideal tropical climate for farming. Wakanda also has advanced farming techniques that make it an ideal location for grafting trees and it is now among the top cultivators.

   This recipe can be made by hand with a whisk; however, by using the blender you can fluff the avocado and create an airier mousse. Dip plantain chips, corn chips, or fresh vegetables like sliced carrots for a snack.

DIFFICULTY: Easy • **PREP TIME:** 10 minutes • **YIELD:** 4 to 6 servings
DIETARY NOTES: Gluten-free, nondairy, nut-free

4 avocados, halved and seeded

2 garlic cloves

½ cup coconut milk

¼ cup lemon juice

1 teaspoon ground cumin

1 teaspoon paprika

Salt

TOOLS:

Blender

1. Scoop out each half of the avocado and cut into halves again. Combine the avocado, garlic, and coconut milk in the blender on high speed to incorporate air, about 2 minutes. It should be light green in color and have small peaks.

2. Transfer blended avocado to a medium-sized mixing bowl and stir in lemon juice, cumin, and paprika.

3. Salt to taste. Garnish with paprika. Serve with Plantain Chips (page 53).

CARDAMOM GRANITA

Sub-Saharan Africa can get very hot, and so many Wakandans make this shaved ice either as a snack on its own or to put on top of other desserts, like mango sorbet.

DIFFICULTY: Easy • **PREP TIME:** 10 minute • **WAIT TIME:** 3 hours
YIELD: 4 servings • **DIETARY NOTES:** Gluten-free, nondairy, nut-free, vegan

2/3 cup cane sugar

1 2/3 cups water

1 tablespoon loose black tea

6 cardamom pods, crushed

1 lemon, zested and juiced

1/2 cup pinapple juice

1. In a small saucepan, bring sugar, 2/3 cup of water, and tea to a boil until the sugar is dissolved, about 2 minutes. Add cardamom pods and lemon zest and steep until the liquid is completely cool.

2. Strain the liquid and mix in the lemon juice, pineapple juice, and 1 cup of water.

3. Pour into a baking dish, cover with plastic, and place in the freezer.

4. Using a fork, scrape and stir the mixture every 30 minutes, gradually creating small crystals of slushy ice, about 3 hours.

5. Granita can be kept stored in the freezer for 3 days.

PILI PILI SAUCE

This sauce is found all over the continent of Africa and beyond. Pili pili refers to any sauce that uses hot chili peppers; it is also known as peri peri sauce. Ideally the African bird's eye chili is used. But habañeros, jalapeños, or serrano peppers can be substituted.

DIFFICULTY: Easy • **PREP TIME:** 10 minutes • **COOK TIME:** 10 minutes
YIELD: 1 cup • **DIETARY NOTES:** Gluten-free, nondairy, vegan

1 tablespoon peanut oil

1 small yellow onion, medium diced

3 garlic cloves, roughly chopped

One 2-inch piece fresh ginger, peeled and roughly chopped

1 vine tomato, roughly chopped

2 bird's eye chiles (or 1 medium serrano pepper)

¼ cup lemon juice

½ cup cider vinegar

¼ cup granulated cane sugar

½ teaspoon salt

TOOLS:
Blender

1. In a small saucepan, heat oil over medium-high heat. Add onion, garlic, ginger, tomato, and chiles.

2. Cook vegetables, stirring occasionally, until onions are translucent, and the peppers are soft, about 3 minutes.

3. Transfer the cooked vegetables to a blender and add lemon juice, vinegar, sugar, and salt. Blend on medium-high until smooth.

4. Cool down and store refrigerated for up to 1 week.

MANGO GEL

Keeping up with modern cooking techniques around the world, the mango gel is used as a plate garnish. You can create decorative dots or swirls, and it tastes good too!

DIFFICULTY: Easy • **PREP TIME:** 5 minutes • **COOK TIME:** 5 minutes
YIELD: 1 cup • **DIETARY NOTES:** Gluten-free, nondairy, nut-free, vegan

1 cup mango juice

1 lemon, juiced

½ teaspoon agar agar

½ teaspoon xantham gum

¼ teaspoon salt

1. In a small saucepan bring ½ cup mango juice, agar agar, xantham, and salt to a boil and remove from heat.

2. Whisk in the remaining mango juice and lemon and transfer to a squeeze bottle.

GINGER GRANITA

Similar to the cardamom granita, this is a shaved ice dish that can be served on its own or as a garnish on top of sorbet.

DIFFICULTY: Easy • **PREP TIME:** 10 minutes • **WAIT TIME:** 6 hours
YIELD: 6 servings • **DIETARY NOTES:** Gluten-free, nondairy, nut-free, vegan

2 cups water

One 2-inch piece fresh ginger, peeled and minced

½ cup granulated cane sugar

1 lemon, juiced

1. In a small saucepan, heat the water, ginger, and sugar. Bring to a boil.

2. Simmer until the sugar is dissolved. Remove from heat.

3. Strain out the ginger, then whisk in the lemon juice.

4. Pour the syrup into a baking pan or plastic container at least ½-inch deep, and place in the freezer.

5. Stir with a fork every hour until ice crystals form.

6. Serve on its own or as a garnish with sorbet.

MARKET
FOOD

Glazed Road Runner Wings

In Wakanda, we call the chickens that we eat "road runners" as slang to mean they are free range and organic. I prefer to smoke the wings for about 20 minutes after brining and before frying, but they taste just as good fried and glazed with the tangy mango ginger sauce.

DIFFICULTY: Easy • **PREP TIME:** 30 minutes • **COOK TIME:** 10 minutes
YIELD: 2 to 3 servings • **DIETARY NOTES:** Gluten-free, nondairy, nut-free

BRINE

¼ cup salt

4 cups water

CHICKEN

1½ pounds chicken wings

2 cups vegetable oil

½ cup Mango Ginger Sauce (page 21)

TOOLS:

Cast-iron skillet

TO MAKE THE BRINE:

1. In a small saucepan, combine salt and 2 cups of water. Bring to a boil over high heat until salt is completely dissolved, about 2 minutes. Transfer to a pitcher and add 2 cups cold water.

TO PREPARE THE CHICKEN:

2. Place wings in a deep pan and pour the brine over.

3. Leave the wings in the brine for 30 minutes refrigerated.

4. Drain wings from brine and pat dry with paper towels.

5. Heat oil in a 2-inch-deep cast-iron skillet. When the oil begins to pop, using a pair of tongs, place wings one at a time into the oil.

6. Cook wings until brown on the outside, about 10 minutes.

7. Remove wings one at a time with tongs and place on a plate or tray with paper towels.

8. In a large mixing bowl, toss cooked wings with the Mango Ginger Sauce.

Lamb Kebabs

Goat is a common meat seen in Wakanda and in surrounding countries. If it cannot be found in your local market, lamb meat is an appropriate substitution. Slow cooking goat or lamb is a tradition that dates back to fifth century Wakanda. My family used braised goat and translated it into market food by serving it on skewers with grilled vegetables. This recipe is great for a party appetizer as well.

DIFFICULTY: Advanced • **PREP TIME:** 40 minutes • **COOK TIME:** 10 minutes
YIELD: 8 portions • **DIETARY NOTES:** Gluten-free, nondairy, nut-free

BRAISE

1 pound lamb stew meat, cut into 1-inch pieces

1 tablespoon cornstarch

1 tablespoon olive oil

1 medium white onion, sliced

1 large carrot, sliced

2 celery stalks, sliced

3 garlic cloves, chopped

1 cup vegetable stock

SKEWERS

1 large bell pepper, diced

1 large white onion, diced

Braising liquid

Braised lamb meat

Salt and pepper

TOOLS:

Grill

Kebab skewers

TO MAKE THE BRAISE:

1. In a medium bowl, toss the lamb meat with the cornstarch and set aside.

2. Heat olive oil in a medium skillet over medium heat and add onion, carrot, celery, and garlic. Sauté, stirring occasionally, until onions become translucent, about 3 minutes.

3. Turn heat up to medium-high and add the lamb meat. Sear the meat until browned on all sides.

4. Add vegetable stock and turn the temperature down to medium-low. Let the meat slowly braise, stirring occasionally.

5. Once the sauce has thickened and the meat is tender to the touch, about 15 minutes, turn off heat. Separate the meat from the stock (saving the liquid for the grilling).

6. Cool the meat for at least 30 minutes or overnight.

7. If serving the same day, the liquid can be kept warm.

TO PREPARE THE SKEWERS:

8. In a medium mixing bowl, toss the pepper and onion with the reserved braising liquid. Salt and pepper to taste.

9. Skewer the kebabs beginning with pepper and alternating meat, onion, meat, pepper, using 3 pieces of meat per skewer.

10. Place skewers on a hot grill and cover, rotating regularly.

11. Skewers are finished when the vegetables have browned on all sides, about 5 to 10 minutes, depending on the heat of your grill.

ZOUMA BOWA

The Dora Milaje were regular customers at my family's market food stand. Eventually Anti Bahiya began to curate snacks for them when traveling and training. She created these smoked, marinated, and then dehydrated mushrooms to resemble a western-style meat jerky. They are a tasty snack for anytime but especially if you find yourself out in the woods for a while.

DIFFICULTY: Advanced • **PREP TIME:** 10 minutes • **COOK TIME:** 5 hours
YIELD: 1 pint • **DIETARY NOTES:** Nondairy, nut-free

1 cup soy sauce

1 cup water

¼ cup rice wine vinegar

½ cup brown sugar

1 tablespoon onion powder

1 tablespoon garlic powder

1 teaspoon ground black pepper

2 pints mushrooms (lion's mane, shiitake, oyster, or pioppini)

TOOLS:

Dehydrator

Smoker

Vacuum sealer

TO MAKE THE MARINADE:

1. In a medium-sized saucepan, bring the soy sauce, water, rice vinegar, brown sugar, onion powder, garlic powder, and black pepper up to a boil over medium-high heat. Once boiling, remove from heat and cool down.

TO PREPARE THE MUSHROOMS:

2. Trim the mushrooms into small clusters and clean off dirt.

3. Smoke mushrooms according to your smoker's directions for 5 to 10 minutes depending on their size, being sure not to cook them but just incorporate the smoke smell. Remove from heat and cool.

4. Place mushrooms in a vacuum seal bag, pour in the marinade, and marinate overnight. If you don't have a vacuum sealer, place mushrooms in a 1-gallon ziplock bag and pour double the amount of marinade on top. Marinate refrigerated overnight, but no more than 2 days.

5. Drain the mushrooms and place in a dehydrator set for 145 degrees Fahrenheit. Let the mushrooms dry out for 3 to 5 hours. They should be chewy and a little tough but not crunchy.

6. Store in an airtight container for up to 2 weeks.

Smoked Chambo

Nyanza is a beautiful body of water that Wakandans source their fish from. Many fishermen use a technique similar to smoking and will sell the chambo whole to the visiting day swimmers. Wakandans do not use fossil fuels for cooking, so I have made some modifications for coal or propane smokers that are commonly found around the world. The smoked fish can be eaten plain as a snack or served with rice and a sauce.

DIFFICULTY: Advanced • **PREP TIME:** 10 minutes • **COOK TIME:** 1 to 1½ hours
YIELD: 2 to 4 servings • **DIETARY NOTES:** Gluten-free, nondairy, nut-free

BRINE

4 cups water

¼ cup kosher salt

FISH

1 whole white fish (such as tilapia, sea bass, or walleye), cleaned and butterflied

TOOLS:

Smoker

TO MAKE THE BRINE:

1. In a small saucepan, bring the water and salt to a boil. Once boiling, remove from heat and cool.

TO PREPARE THE FISH:

2. Make one incision in the fish on the bottom belly side from head to tail. Use your knife to separate one side of the rib bones so that the fish lays out like a butterfly.

3. Brine the fish in a ziplock bag for 30 minutes.

4. Drain the fish and lightly rinse with cold water.

5. Place on smoker skin side down and cook until the flesh is golden brown, about 1 to 1½ hours.

CHICKEN MEATBALLS

This recipe began as a snack for me when I was a little girl and working with my mother at the market. Now I serve it as an appetizer at parties the royal family throws whenever there is a new class of Dora Milaje being initiated. We serve them with a side of the warmed msuzi matimati sauce. The Dora Milaje often go on to purchase the meatballs from my mother at her stand when they have breaks from training.

DIFFICULTY: Medium • **PREP TIME:** 20 minutes • **COOK TIME:** 10 minutes
YIELD: 10 servings • **DIETARY NOTES:** Gluten-free, nondairy

1 pound ground chicken

2 small limes, zested and juiced

1 teaspoon Harissa Spice Mix (page 27)

1 teaspoon kosher salt

1 teaspoon garlic powder

½ teaspoon ground coriander

TOOLS:

Grill

1. In a large mixing bowl, combine all the ingredients until fully incorporated.

2. Using a 1-inch ice cream scoop or a large soup spoon, form out approximately 1-inch balls.

3. Cook over a greased grill for 3 minutes on each side, or until each side has grill marks.

4. Serve with Msuzi Matimati (page 29) or Muhammara (page 19).

Vegetable Samosas

Samosas truly are a delicious and versatile snack. This meatless version includes peas and some vegetable stock and curry powder to spice up the rest of the vegetables. I have modified this recipe to use spring roll wrappers because in all my travels and tasting of samosas, I love a crispy crust the best.

Difficulty: Medium • **Prep Time:** 10 minutes • **Cook Time:** 20 minutes
Yield: 2 to 4 servings • **Dietary Notes:** Nondairy, nut-free, vegetarian

1 tablespoon peanut oil

1 medium carrot, small diced

2 celery stalks, small diced

1 small yellow onion, small diced

2 small russet potatoes, small diced

2 cups peas

1 cup vegetable stock

¼ cup lemon juice

2 tablespoons yellow curry powder

1 teaspoon ground ginger

1 teaspoon ground black pepper

1 teaspoon crushed chiles

1 teaspoon onion powder

2 teaspoons garlic powder

1 tablespoon salt

2 bay leaves

20 sheets of 5-inch spring roll pastry wrappers

Water for sealing wrappers

2 cups vegetable oil

TO MAKE THE FILLING:

1. In a medium saucepan, heat peanut oil over medium heat. Add carrot, celery, onion, and potatoes. Cook for 4 minutes, stirring occasionally.

2. Add peas, vegetable stock, lemon juice, curry powder, ginger, black pepper, chiles, onion powder, garlic powder, salt, and bay leaves. Mix together in the pan, cover, and simmer for 10 minutes.

3. Remove filling from heat, transfer to a baking pan to cool, and remove the bay leaves.

TO FOLD THE SAMOSAS:

4. Cut each spring roll wrapper into 3 equal rectangles going vertically. Stack the rectangles and cover with a damp paper towel while folding to keep the wrappers from drying out.

5. Take the first rectangle piece and place it on a cutting board horizontally. Take the bottom right corner of the rectangle and fold it across to the left to form the first triangle for the pocket for the filling.

6. Take the top of the new triangle and fold it down and across to the left, aligning it with the flat bottom, making a new layer for the pocket.

7. Pick up the wrapper pocket and spoon in 1 tablespoon of filling.

8. Fold the pocket across to the left again, leaving a short rectangle.

9. To seal off the wrapper, pat a small amount of water on the end and fold over.

10. Repeat until you have used up all the filling.

TO COOK THE SAMOSAS:

11. Heat vegetable oil in a frying pan to 350 degrees Fahrenheit.

12. Fry the samosas until brown on each side, about 3 minutes.

BEEF SAMOSAS

Samosas are one of the most common snacks seen on menus across Wakanda. It was not until I began to work for the royal family and left home that I learned that they are also traditional in India and Pakistan. Through travel and food, I have been able to see how the world is connected, and the tiny glimpses of Wakanda are everywhere, as my Anti Bahiya told me.

DIFFICULTY: Medium • **PREP TIME:** 10 minutes • **COOK TIME:** 20 minutes
YIELD: 10 servings • **DIETARY NOTES:** Nondairy

1 tablespoon peanut oil

1 medium carrot, small diced

2 celery stalks, small diced

1 small yellow onion, small diced

1 small russet potato, small diced

1 pound ground beef

¼ cup lemon juice

1 teaspoon ground ginger

1 teaspoon ground cumin

1 teaspoon ground black pepper

1 teaspoon crushed chiles

1 teaspoon onion powder

2 teaspoons garlic powder

¼ cup white vinegar

¼ cup brown sugar

1 tablespoon salt

2 bay leaves

20 sheets of 5-inch spring roll pastry wrappers

Water for sealing wrappers

2 cups vegetable oil

TO MAKE THE FILLING:

1. In a medium saucepan, heat peanut oil over medium heat. Add carrot, celery, onion, and potato. Cook for 4 minutes, stirring occasionally.

2. Add ground beef and cook until browned, stirring often to break up the meat.

3. Once the meat is browned, add lemon juice, ginger, cumin, black pepper, chiles, onion powder, garlic powder, vinegar, brown sugar, salt, and bay leaves. Mix in the pan, cover, and simmer for 20 minutes.

4. Remove filling from heat, transfer to a baking pan to cool, and remove the bay leaves.

TO FOLD THE SAMOSAS:

5. Cut each spring roll wrapper into 3 equal rectangles going vertically. Stack the rectangles and cover with a damp towel while folding to keep the wrappers from drying out.

6. Take the first rectangle piece and place it on a cutting board horizontally. Take the bottom right corner of the rectangle and fold it across to the left to form the first triangle for the pocket for the filling.

7. Take the top of the new triangle and fold it down and across to the left, aligning it with the flat bottom, making a new layer for the pocket.

8. Pick up the wrapper pocket and spoon in 1 tablespoon of filling.

9. Fold the pocket across to the left again, leaving a short rectangle.

10. To seal off the wrapper, pat a small amount of water on the end and fold over.

11. Repeat until you have used up all the filling.

TO COOK THE SAMOSAS:

12. Heat vegetable oil in a frying pan to 350 degrees Fahrenheit.

13. Fry the samosas until brown on each side, about 3 minutes.

GRILLED CHIMANGA WITH CURRIED AIOLI

Part of Wakandan culture is cultivation. Chimanga (also known as maize or corn) is grown in most of our yards. We eat it fresh off the stalk or mill it into flour. At the family food stand we would keep the husk on while grilling so it would have a natural holder. Seasoning the chimanga with the aioli before grilling creates a crispy and caramelized crust.

DIFFICULTY: Easy • **PREP TIME:** 10 minutes • **COOK TIME:** 10 minutes
YIELD: 4 servings • **DIETARY NOTES:** Gluten-free, nondairy, vegetarian

4 ears corn on the cob

1 cup Curried Aioli (page 23)

¼ cup Harissa Spice Mix (page 27)

TOOLS:

Grill

1. To clean the corn, peel the outer layer of the husk and discard. Be sure to save at least one layer, if not more, of the husk to use as the handle while eating the corn.

2. Peel the remaining husk back and down, out of the way. Using your hands pick off the white silk and discard.

3. Spread ¼ cup of Curried Aioli on each of the corn on the cobs, covering all sides.

4. Place corn on the cobs on a hot grill and cook, rotating until all sides have a golden-brown color.

5. Garnish with a sprinkle of the Harissa Spice Mix.

PLANTAIN CHIPS

For those of us Wakandans that travel, we enjoy dining at restaurants that feature foods from the African diaspora. There is a Jamaican restaurant in Brooklyn that features many of the same flavors as Wakanda food. The Dora Milajae and I often enjoy visiting and ordering the plantain chips. They are long and thin and crispy and are often served with a variety of dips and salsas.

DIFFICULTY: Easy • **PREP TIME:** 5 minutes • **COOK TIME:** 5 minutes
YIELD: 4 to 6 servings • **DIETARY NOTES:** Gluten-free, nondairy, nut-free, vegan

4 green plantains

2 cups vegetable oil

Kosher salt

TOOLS:

Cast-iron skillet or Dutch oven

1. Cut off the ends of the plantains and peel.

2. Using a vegetable peeler or mandoline, slice the plantains thinly lengthwise.

3. In a cast-iron skillet or Dutch oven, heat the oil to 350 degrees Fahrenheit.

4. Drop the slices of plantains into the hot oil, about 3 to 4 at a time.

5. Fry the slices until they become crispy and golden brown on both sides, about 1 to 2 minutes.

6. Remove from oil and drain on paper towels.

7. Season with salt.

8. Serve chips with Muhammara (page 19), Chinananzi Salsa (page 20), or Peyala Mousse (page 31).

OKRA FRITTERS

The okra fritters were one of the most popular items on the family food stand menu from before I was born. Fritters are commonly seen throughout Wakanda and this version uses two of the country's greatest crops, okra and corn.

DIFFICULTY: Easy • **PREP TIME:** 10 minutes • **COOK TIME:** 10 minutes
YIELD: 4 servings • **DIETARY NOTES:** Nut-free, vegetarian

1 egg

¼ cup goat's milk (or whole cow's milk)

½ cup all-purpose flour

¼ cup cornmeal

1 teaspoon garlic powder

1 teaspoon smoked paprika

1 teaspoon onion powder

1 teaspoon salt

1 teaspoon ground black pepper

1 cup thinly sliced fresh okra (or frozen okra pieces, thawed)

1 cup corn kernels

2 cups vegetable oil

1. In a medium mixing bowl, whisk the egg with goat's milk.

2. In a separate bowl, combine flour, cornmeal, garlic powder, smoked paprika, onion powder, salt, and pepper.

3. Pour egg mixture into flour mixture and mix with a spatula.

4. Fold in the okra and corn.

5. Heat oil in a large skillet to 325 degrees Fahrenheit.

6. Using a large soupspoon, drop spoonfuls of the batter into the hot oil. Use a slotted spoon or spatula to turn the fritters until they are brown on all sides, about 2 to 3 minutes.

7. Remove from oil and cool on paper towels.

8. Serve on their own or with the Curried Aioli (page 23), Muhammara (page 19), or Chinananzi Salsa (page 20).

Harissa Spiced Popcorn

Although education and learning were heavily pushed in the Royal Palace, when Princess Shuri and King T'Challa were young children, they were granted movie nights from time to time. They always watched the newest films on the newest screening equipment that was being tested. On those evenings I would use our air popper and make them this treat. I would serve it with the homemade tamarind cola. This popcorn recipe has been modified for popping the kernels over a common home stove.

DIFFICULTY: Easy • **COOK TIME:** 10 minutes
YIELD: 4 servings • **DIETARY NOTES:** Gluten-free, nut-free, vegetarian

1 cup coconut oil

⅓ cup popcorn kernels

1 tablespoon Harissa Spice Mix (page 27)

1 tablespoon nutritional yeast

1 teaspoon salt

1. Melt coconut oil in a thick bottomed medium-sized saucepan on medium-high heat.

2. Pour the kernels into the pot and cover. As the kernels begin to pop gently, shake the pan holding on to the lid. As the popping starts to slow down, remove the pot from heat.

3. In a small mixing bowl combine Harissa Spice Mix, nutritional yeast, and salt.

4. Toss the popped kernels with the spices.

BOILED MTEDZA

Boiling mtedza, or groundnuts, such as peanuts, is very inherently African. You will find this preparation all across Wakanda. I was shocked to learn that boiled peanuts can be found throughout the world. After some research I discovered that it was the enslaved Africans who were brought to America that also brought with them this tradition of boiling groundnuts. This snack is best enjoyed with a tamarind cola.

DIFFICULTY: Easy • **COOK TIME:** 10 minutes
YIELD: 4 servings • **DIETARY NOTES:** Gluten-free, vegetarian

1 pound raw or dried peanuts in shells

6 curry leaves

3 tablespoons salt

Water to cover peanuts, about 12 cups

1. Rinse the peanuts in a strainer and transfer to a large stockpot.

2. Add curry leaves, salt, and water.

3. Cover and bring to a boil over high heat.

4. Reduce heat to medium and simmer covered until the peanuts are soft, about 3 hours.

5. Remove the pot from heat and strain the peanuts.

6. Enjoy them warm or chilled. To eat, pinch one end of the shell to pop out the peanut flesh. Some people also like to slurp the liquid in the shell. Discard the shell and repeat.

7. The peanuts can be stored refrigerated for up to 6 days.

Cassava Fries

While the Western world prefers potatoes for making fries, in Wakanda we utilize the magnificent cassava. You can find fried cassava root at outdoor markets across the country and it is often served in Wakandan homes for every meal. Try serving these with spiced ketchup. These were definitely a dish that young T'Challa and Shuri enjoyed with their breakfast eggs.

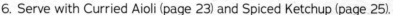

DIFFICULTY: Easy • **PREP TIME:** 5 minutes • **COOK TIME:** 5 minutes
YIELD: 4 to 6 servings • **DIETARY NOTES:** Gluten-free, nondairy, nut-free, vegan

3 pounds cassava root, also known as yuca

2 cups vegetable oil

Salt

TOOLS:

Dutch oven

1. Cut the ends off of the cassava, peel, and cut out the core.

2. Cut the cassava into 2-inch pieces.

3. Heat oil in the Dutch oven to 350 degrees Fahrenheit.

4. Fry the cassava pieces until golden on each side, about 3 to 5 minutes.

5. Remove from oil with a slotted spoon. Dry and drain on paper towels. Salt to taste.

6. Serve with Curried Aioli (page 23) and Spiced Ketchup (page 25).

BREAKFAST

Baked Sweet Potato and Kale Eggs

A breakfast suitable for kings. King T'Challa in fact. The sweet potato can be roasted ahead of time and then gently reheated or served at room temperature. Mixing the kale pesto with the eggs makes them appetizingly green!

DIFFICULTY: Easy • **PREP TIME:** 5 minutes • **COOK TIME:** 45 minutes
YIELD: 4 servings • **DIETARY NOTES:** Gluten-free, nondairy, nut-free

1 large sweet potato

4 eggs, scrambled

3 teaspoons vegetable oil

1 teaspoon salt

1 teaspoon pepper

2 tablespoons Kale Pesto (page 26)

1. To roast the sweet potato, preheat the oven to 375 degrees.

2. Coat the sweet potato with 1 tablespoon of the vegetable oil, as well as 1 teaspoon each of salt and pepper, and place on a foil-lined baking sheet.

3. With a fork, poke a few holes in the sweet potato. Bake in the oven until tender and the skin begins to get crisp, about 30 minutes.

4. In a nonstick sauté pan, heat the remaining 2 tablespoons of vegetable oil.

5. Add the Kale Pesto and cook for 30 seconds.

6. Whisk in the eggs until they're incorporated with the pesto. Remove from heat.

7. To serve, cut the sweet potato in half lengthwise, and then cut each half again, crosswise.

8. Top each piece of sweet potato with a spoonful of egg scramble.

9. Add salt and pepper to taste.

RICE PORRIDGE

There are two ways to enjoy a rice porridge: sweet or savory. Some Wakandans enjoy their breakfast porridge sweet with brown sugar, butter, and a little cinnamon. Others enjoy it with braised meats like lamb and a sous vide egg and hot sauce. If you don't have a sous vide machine, you can easily substitute it with a poached egg.

DIFFICULTY: Medium • **PREP TIME:** 5 minutes • **COOK TIME:** 30 minutes
YIELD: 4 servings • **DIETARY NOTES:** Gluten-free, nondairy, nut-free

PORRIDGE

1 cup white rice

6 cups water

½ teaspoon salt

1 tablespoon unsalted butter

SWEET

1 tablespoon granulated cane sugar

½ teaspoon ground nutmeg

½ teaspoon ground cinnamon

SAVORY

1 cup braised lamb (see Lamb Kebabs, page 41)

4 eggs

4 tablespoons Pili Pili Sauce (page 34)

4 tablespoons Kale Pesto (page 26)

Salt

TO MAKE THE PORRIDGE:

1. Place the rice in a fine mesh strainer and rinse until the water runs clear.

2. Transfer the strained rice to a medium stockpot with 6 cups of water and salt.

3. Bring the water to a boil and then reduce to medium heat.

4. Cook the rice, stirring occasionally, until the rice is thick and sticky, about 30 to 40 minutes.

5. Turn off heat and mix in butter.

FOR A SWEET PORRIDGE:

6. Mix in sugar, nutmeg, and cinnamon. Divide into bowls.

FOR A SAVORY PORRIDGE:

7. Salt the rice to taste and divide into bowls.

8. Warm the lamb meat over the stovetop and portion evenly among the bowls.

9. One at a time, crack the egg into a small bowl. Bring a small saucepan filled with water to a boil.

10. Drop 1 egg in the boiling water and stir occasionally with a slotted spoon until the egg is poached, about 2 minutes. Turn down the heat and remove the egg with the slotted spoon and place on top of the bowl of rice. Repeat with the other 3 eggs.

11. Garnish each bowl with a tablespoon of Pili Pili Sauce and Kale Pesto.

Braised Beans

Many Wakandans start a pot of beans with tomatoes and curry leaves in the morning. For the first meal it is served with tomato sauce, eggs, and toast. Any leftovers can stay over a low heat and are meant to be eaten as a side dish for the rest of the day.

DIFFICULTY: Easy • **PREP TIME:** Overnight • **COOK TIME:** 1 hour
YIELD: 4 to 6 servings • **DIETARY NOTES:** Gluten-free, nondairy, nut-free, vegan

2 cups dried kidney beans

1 teaspoon vegetable oil

1 small yellow onion, small diced

2 tablespoons tomato paste

2 tablespoons brown sugar

1 teaspoon garlic powder

1 teaspoon paprika

1 teaspoon dried oregano

2 cups water

Salt

1. Place the beans in a medium-sized bowl and cover with water. Soak overnight.

2. In a medium saucepan, heat the oil on medium heat.

3. Add the onion and cook for 2 minutes, stirring occasionally.

4. Add the tomato paste, sugar, garlic powder, paprika, and oregano and mix together. Salt to taste.

5. Slowly add the water until fully incorporated.

6. Simmer the beans on medium-high heat for 1 hour, or until soft and tender.

7. Serve on the side with eggs and tomato sauce.

AKARA

In villages across Wakanda and even among the young professionals of the larger cities, akara is made as a quick and easy transportable breakfast food. A traditional breakfast is not complete without a plate full of akara. Akara is a fried bean fritter that is usually served at breakfast but can really be enjoyed at any time of the day. Dip it in a sauce like msuzi matimati or eat them warm out of the pan.

DIFFICULTY: Medium • **PREP TIME:** 5 minutes • **WAIT TIME:** 24 hours • **COOK TIME:** 5 minutes
YIELD: 4 to 6 servings • **DIETARY NOTES:** Gluten-free, nondairy, nut-free, vegan

2 cups dried black-eyed peas (or one 15-ounce can cooked black-eyed peas)

Water to cover black-eyed peas

1 teaspoon salt

1 habañero pepper

1 small yellow onion

¾ cup cassava flour

2 cups vegetable oil

TOOLS:

Blender

Dutch oven

1. Place the black-eyed peas in a medium pot and cover with water so that the water is 2 inches above the peas.

2. Stir in the salt and soak the beans overnight.

3. Peel the beans by rubbing the skins off underwater and drain off.

4. Transfer the peas to a blender and purée with pepper and onion.

5. Blend until smooth and resembles a batter, about 4 minutes.

6. Transfer the batter to a medium-sized bowl and mix in the cassava flour.

7. Heat the oil in a Dutch oven to 350 degrees Fahrenheit.

8. Using a large soupspoon, drop spoonfuls of the batter into the hot oil and fry until golden brown on all sides.

9. Drain on a paper towel.

HARISSA EGGS AND SHAVED CUCUMBERS

Another common breakfast in the Royal Palace household. Princess Shuri enjoys her eggs cooked soft and so I came up with a recipe that features the eggs. It is best to enjoy them with a crisp piece of lavash and sprinkled with a little of the harissa spice mix.

DIFFICULTY: Easy • **PREP TIME:** 10 minutes • **COOK TIME:** 6 minutes
YIELD: 4 servings • **DIETARY NOTES:** Gluten-free, Nondairy, nut-free

4 eggs

1 large cucumber

1 small onion, thinly sliced

2 tablespoons Carrot Ginger Dressing (page 24)

1 tablespoon Harissa Spice Mix (page 27)

1. To boil the eggs, bring a large saucepan of water to a boil. Using a slotted spoon, gently place the eggs in the boiling water.

2. Boil the eggs for 6½ minutes. While the eggs are cooking, add iced water to a medium bowl.

3. Immediately transfer the eggs to the bowl of iced water and let cool.

4. Trim the ends of the cucumber.

5. Using a vegetable peeler, make thin slices lengthwise around the cucumber.

6. In a small mixing bowl, combine the onion, cucumber, and Carrot Ginger Dressing, and mix until the vegetables are coated. Cover and chill for 5 minutes.

7. Gently peel the eggs and slice them each in half lengthwise.

8. Place the eggs on a serving platter and sprinkle the Harissa Spice Mix and a pinch of salt over the yolks. Place the chilled cucumbers next to the eggs.

9. Enjoy with a side of Lavash (Page 97).

Sweet Potato Granola

Granola is another food that King T'Challa discovered while studying abroad. Once the granola mixture is baked it can be stored and eaten plain or on top of yogurt made from goat's milk or in a bowl with goat's or cow's milk.

DIFFICULTY: Medium • **PREP TIME:** 15 minutes • **COOK TIME:** 1½ hours
YIELD: 4 to 6 servings • **DIETARY NOTES:** Gluten-free, nondairy

1 large sweet potato

3 cups rolled oats

½ cup coconut oil

½ cup honey

1 teaspoon ground cinnamon

¼ teaspoon ground ginger

¼ teaspoon ground nutmeg

½ teaspoon salt

1 teaspoon vanilla extract

1 cup pecans, chopped

TOOLS:

Blender

1. Preheat the oven to 350 degrees Fahrenheit.

2. Using a fork, poke the sweet potato twice and place on a baking sheet. Bake the sweet potato until soft, about 30 minutes. Remove from the oven, scoop the flesh from the skin, and set aside to cool.

3. Lower the heat of the oven to 300 degrees Fahrenheit.

4. On a parchment-lined baking tray, lay out the oats into a single layer and toast until aromatic, about 10 minutes. Remove from the oven and let cool slightly.

5. In the blender, combine the cooked sweet potato, coconut oil, honey, cinnamon, ginger, nutmeg, salt, and vanilla and mix on high for 2 minutes.

6. Transfer the sweet potato mixture to a large mixing bowl and combine with the pecans and toasted oats.

7. Spread the mixture out onto the parchment-lined baking tray into a single layer and bake for 30 to 40 minutes.

8. Let the granola cool and store in an airtight container for up to 3 weeks.

Carob Energy Balls

This was a recipe that Anti Bahiya helped me develop. It is inspired by one of the snacks served at the Dora Milaje Training Center. During their training period the Dora Milaje are on a special diet to give them energy and strength.

DIFFICULTY: Easy • **PREP TIME:** 10 minutes • **WAIT TIME:** 30 minutes
YIELD: 4 to 6 servings • **DIETARY NOTES:** Gluten-free, nondairy, nut-free

1 cup rolled oats

1 cup peanut butter

¼ cup flax seed powder

½ cup carob chips

½ cup shredded unsweetened coconut

½ cup honey

½ teaspoon vanilla extract

1. In a large mixing bowl, combine oats, peanut butter, flax seed, carob chips, coconut, honey, and vanilla.

2. Using a 1-inch cookie scoop, portion out balls and roll in your palm to firm the balls.

3. Once all the batter is rolled out, refrigerate the balls for at least 30 minutes to form.

4. Store in an airtight container for up to 1 week or store frozen for up to 1 month.

SOUPS AND SALADS

OKRA AND BEEF SOUP

We use okuru (okra) in many of our soups and stews because it works as a thickener. During the rainy seasons this simple soup becomes a comfort food for Wakandans.

DIFFICULTY: Easy • **PREP TIME:** 5 minutes • **COOK TIME:** 40 minutes
YIELD: 4 to 6 servings • **DIETARY NOTES:** Gluten-free, Nondairy

3 tablespoons peanut oil

1 medium yellow onion, thinly sliced

2 medium carrots, sliced into rounds

2 celery stalks, sliced

3 garlic cloves, minced

1 pound ground beef

1 teaspoon crushed dried chile pepper

2 cups thinly sliced kale

4 cups vegetable stock

Salt and pepper

1. In a medium stockpot, heat peanut oil over medium heat.

2. Add onion, carrots, celery, and garlic cloves. Cook until the vegetables are translucent and soft, about 3 minutes.

3. Add ground beef and stir with vegetables until the beef is completely browned, about 5 minutes.

4. Add chile pepper, kale, and vegetable stock.

5. Simmer soup for 40 minutes. Salt and pepper to taste. Serve immediately with Lavash (page 97) and Tomato and Herb Salad (page 76).

TOMATO AND HERB SALAD

Chunks of tomato and cucumbers, slices of onion, and freshly picked herbs from the garden are a common side dish for breakfast. It works with a light dressing or sometimes I just toss them in a bowl with lemon juice, salt, and pepper. Enjoy on the side with eggs and toast in the morning.

DIFFICULTY: Easy • **PREP TIME:** 10 minutes
YIELD: 4 servings • **DIETARY NOTES:** Gluten-free, nondairy, nut-free, vegan

2 pounds tomatoes (heirloom or vine), chopped into ½-inch chunks

1 cucumber, chopped into ½-inch chunks

1 small yellow onion, thinly sliced

2 tablespoons olive oil

¼ cup fresh lemon juice

1 tablespoon fresh chives, minced

1 tablespoon fresh mint, minced

1 tablespoon fresh cilantro, minced

1 tablespoon fresh parsley, minced

1 teaspoon salt

1. Chop the tomatoes, cucumber, and onion.

2. In a medium mixing bowl, coat the tomatoes, cucumber, and onion with the oil and lemon juice.

3. Add the herbs and salt and mix with the vegetables.

4. Serve the salad chilled.

Citrus and Avocado Salad

This salad can be plated individually or family style. I like to alternate the fruits when arranging them over the lettuce to create a colorful pattern. The avocados add a rich, creamy component that is balanced by the toasted pumpkin seeds.

DIFFICULTY: Medium • **PREP TIME:** 10 minutes
YIELD: 3 to 4 servings • **DIETARY NOTES:** Gluten-free, nondairy, nut-free

2 blood oranges, peeled and sliced into ¼-inch rounds

2 navel oranges, peeled and sliced into ¼-inch rounds

1 pink grapefruit, peeled and sliced into ¼-inch rounds

2 limes, peeled and sliced into ¼-inch rounds

2 cups Bibb or Boston hydroponic lettuce, leaves kept whole

3 tablespoons Carrot Ginger Dressing (page 24)

2 avocados, peeled and sliced into ¼-inch strips

¼ cup pepitas (pumpkin seeds), chopped

1. With a paring knife, cut the ends off the blood oranges, navel oranges, grapefruit, and limes. Use the knife to peel the skin off from top to bottom. Slice the citrus horizontally to make rounds. Set aside.

2. In a small mixing bowl, toss the lettuce with the Carrot Ginger Dressing. Make a layer of the greens on the serving plate.

3. Toss the citrus in the same mixing bowl with the dressing. Arrange the citrus over the lettuce.

4. Arrange the avocados evenly on top of the citrus.

5. Garnish with the chopped pepitas.

Chilled Watermelon Soup

There is nothing like a cold slice of watermelon on a hot day. This soup incorporates that experience with puréed melon, bread, and lemon juice. When King T'Challa was in America for his studies he came across this chilled watermelon soup at a restaurant and upon his return to Wakanda requested that we create a version.

DIFFICULTY: Easy ● **PREP TIME:** 10 minutes
YIELD: 4 to 6 servings ● **DIETARY NOTES:** Nondairy, nut-free, vegan

2 cups country-style bread loaf, torn into ½-inch pieces

4 cups watermelon juice (about 1 small watermelon, puréed in juicer/blender and strained)

½ cup tomato water (about 2 to 3 tomatoes, puréed and strained)

½ teaspoon ground cayenne pepper

¼ cup sherry vinegar

⅛ cup lemon juice

½ cup olive oil

Salt and pepper

TOOLS:

Blender

1. Soak the bread in the watermelon juice and tomato water for 1 hour, or until the bread is soft.

2. Transfer the bread, watermelon juice, and tomato water to a blender. Purée with cayenne, vinegar, and lemon juice.

3. Slowly add the olive oil while blending to create an emulsion.

4. Salt and pepper to taste. Serve chilled.

KABICHI

When my mother and anti first began their business, the first dish they served was a curried chicken stew with nsima and a side of this cabbage salad. Their version dressed the cabbage with peanut oil and vinegars, however I have updated the recipe so that all of the vegetables have to be sliced very thin and tossed with the curried aioli. It is the perfect side to any braised meat.

DIFFICULTY: Easy • **PREP TIME:** 20 minutes
YIELD: 4 to 6 servings • **DIETARY NOTES:** Gluten-free, nut-free

1 small green cabbage, thinly sliced

2 large carrots, thinly sliced into matchsticks

1 large yellow onion, thinly sliced

1 large red bell pepper, thinly sliced

½ cup fresh cilantro, chopped

1 lemon, juiced

1 cup Curried Aioli (page 23)

¼ cup apple cider vinegar

1 teaspoon mustard powder

Salt and pepper

1. Slice the cabbage, carrots, onion, and pepper into even pieces. Toss together in a large bowl and set aside.

2. In another large mixing bowl, combine the cilantro, lemon juice, aioli, cider vinegar, and mustard powder. Salt and pepper to taste.

3. Mix the vegetables with the aioli dressing.

4. Cover and chill for 15 minutes.

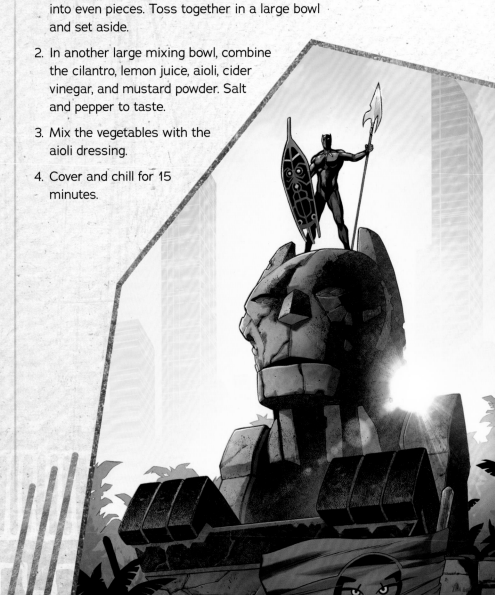

CHIMANGA AND BLACK-EYED PEAS

Chimanga (corn) is harvested and then turned into various food products. For this recipe you make a patty with cooked corn meal and then top it with a cold bean and corn kernel salad. Top it with a fried egg and you also have the perfect breakfast.

DIFFICULTY: Easy • **PREP TIME:** 20 minutes • **WAIT TIME:** 30 minutes
YIELD: 4 to 6 servings • **DIETARY NOTES:** Gluten-free, nondairy, nut-free, vegan

2 cups dried black-eyed peas (or 4 cups cooked)

2 ears corn, kernels cut from cob

1 large red bell pepper, small diced

1 large green bell pepper, small diced

1 medium red onion, small diced

2 serrano peppers (or 1 habañero pepper), seeded and small diced

1 cucumber, peeled and small diced

1 cup fresh parsley, chopped

2 limes, juiced

¼ cup rice wine vinegar

¼ cup olive oil

Salt and pepper

1. If using dried beans, place them in a medium soup pot, cover with water, and add a pinch of salt. Let soak overnight.

2. Drain and rinse the beans and place back in the pot. Cover the beans with 2 inches of water. Simmer over medium-high heat until cooked through, about 1 hour. Drain and set aside to cool.

3. On a cutting board, stand an ear of corn vertically and use a knife to carefully slice down and cut the kernels off.

4. In a large bowl, combine the fresh corn kernels, cooked black-eyed peas, bell peppers, onion, serrano peppers, cucumber, parsley, lime juice, vinegar, and olive oil. Salt and pepper to taste.

5. Mix well, cover, and refrigerate for at least 30 minutes.

MANGO AND PINEAPPLE SALAD

This is a simple recipe that combines some of our most bountiful fruits found in Wakanda and is perfect for a party. By slicing the pineapples into rounds they function as an edible utensil. Pickled red onion and mustard seeds add texture.

DIFFICULTY: Easy • **PREP TIME:** 20 minutes • **WAIT TIME:** 30 minutes
YIELD: 2 to 4 servings • **DIETARY NOTES:** Gluten-free, vegan

½ pineapple, peeled and cut into ¼-inch rounds

2 mangoes, sliced

1 avocado, sliced

¼ cup Carrot Ginger Dressing (page 24)

½ cup roasted peanuts, chopped

¼ cup Mango Gel, in a squeeze bottle (page 35)

1. Cut the top and bottom off of the pineapple and then peel around from top to bottom.

2. Slice the pineapple horizontally into thin rounds.

3. In a large mixing bowl, combine pineapple, mangoes, avocado, and Carrot Ginger Dressing.

4. Place the pineapple rounds on the serving tray.

5. Next, place 2 slices of mango on top of each pineapple round.

6. Top the mango with 1 slice of avocado each.

7. Garnish each serving with chopped roasted peanuts and 3 to 5 drops of the Mango Gel.

PUMPKIN AND CASSAVA LEAF SOUP

Roasted chunks of pumpkin are simmered in a vegetable broth with cassava leaves. If you can't find cassava leaves, fresh or frozen spinach can be a good substitute. Soups are a common meal for farming families to have because we can let the pot sit and simmer while we work the fields. The various types of squashes that can be used all have a tender and mild skin that does not eed to be peeled and they also have a flesh that cooks and softens when left to simmer in a broth. When the chunks of squash start to break apart, the starch helps to create a flavorful broth.

DIFFICULTY: Easy • **PREP TIME:** 10 minutes • **COOK TIME:** 50 minutes
YIELD: 4 to 6 servings • **DIETARY NOTES:** Gluten-free, nondairy, vegan

1 medium pumpkin or squash (acorn, butternut, kabocha)

4 tablespoons peanut oil

1 medium yellow onion, sliced

½ cup peanut butter

¼ cup Pili Pili Sauce (page 34)

1 lemon, juiced

4 cups vegetable broth

3 pounds cassava leaves, cooked (or spinach)

Salt and pepper

1. Preheat the oven to 375 degrees Fahrenheit.

2. Cut the pumpkin in half and the halves into quarters.

3. In a large bowl, toss the pumpkin pieces with 2 tablespoons of peanut oil. Salt and pepper to taste.

4. Lay out the seasoned pumpkin on a foil-lined baking tray.

5. Bake the pumpkin until caramelized and tender, about 45 minutes.

6. In a large stockpot, heat 2 tablespoons of peanut oil with the sliced onion over medium heat.

7. Sauté the onions until translucent, about 4 minutes.

8. Add the peanut butter, Pili Pili Sauce, and lemon juice.

9. Whisk in the vegetable broth.

10. Add the cassava leaves, turn the heat up to high, and bring to a boil. Reduce heat and simmer for 20 to 30 minutes.

11. Turn the heat off and mix in the cooked pumpkin.

12. Salt and pepper to taste.

13. Serve with warm rice.

Vegetables and Sides

BRAISED KALE AND TOMATOES

This is a dish that my mother would make for my family and that she eventually taught to me. Some nights I would sit outside with her by the fire and help her cut the tomatoes and pick the kale. I loved the way the greens would shrink as she added each handful and slowly turned them in the pot. We would eat them with roasted fish and nsima soaking up the vegetable stock with each bite.

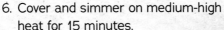

DIFFICULTY: Easy • **PREP TIME:** 10 minutes • **COOK TIME:** 20 minutes
YIELD: 4 servings • **DIETARY NOTES:** Gluten-free, nut-free, vegetarian

2 tablespoons olive oil

1 small yellow onion, sliced

5 garlic cloves, minced

2 vine tomatoes, diced

1 teaspoon ground cumin

1 tablespoon paprika

8 cups curly kale, chopped

1 cup vegetable stock

Salt and pepper

1. Heat oil in a medium sauté pan over medium heat.

2. Add onion and garlic. Cook until onions are translucent, about 4 minutes.

3. Add tomatoes, cumin, and paprika. Salt and pepper to taste.

4. Slowly add the kale, wilting handfuls at a time.

5. Once all of the kale is added to the pot, pour in the vegetable stock.

6. Cover and simmer on medium-high heat for 15 minutes.

CHARRED OKURU

Okuru, or okra, as it is known in English, is seen across the continent of Africa and is used in many different dishes. This is a simple recipe that quickly cooks the okra in boiling water and then finishes them over an open flame. This is a great appetizer when served on skewers with dipping sauces like curried aioli or muhammara.

DIFFICULTY: Easy • **PREP TIME:** 5 minutes
YIELD: 10 servings • **DIETARY NOTES:** Gluten-free, nondairy, nut-free, vegan

One 12-ounce package fresh whole okra

2 tablespoons peanut oil

1 tablespoon nutritional yeast

Salt and pepper

1 lemon, for garnish

TOOLS:

Grill

1. Blanch okra in a large stock pot of salted boiling water for 2 minutes.

2. Transfer to a medium-sized mixing bowl and toss the okra with the peanut oil.

3. Cook okra over a hot grill until each side has grill marks and a little char.

4. Transfer back to the mixing bowl and toss with nutritional yeast. Salt and pepper to taste.

5. Serve with lemon wedges and Curried Aioli (page 23).

SOUS VIDE TUBERS

Sweet potatoes, yams, potatoes, and pumpkin are all referred to as tubers in Wakanda. By slicing them evenly and lightly seasoning them they can be vacuum sealed and cooked to perfect tenderness by using a sous vide technique. Once you have cooked the vegetables in the bag, you can either serve them immediately or chill the bag and save for later. The cooked tubers can be stored in the bag for up to four days. Many working families use the sous vide technique to prepare vegetables in advance. I like to have them on hand in case Shuri shows up with a guest like Iron Man.

DIFFICULTY: Easy • **PREP TIME:** 10 minutes • **COOK TIME:** 20 minutes
YIELD: 4 to 6 servings • **DIETARY NOTES:** Gluten-free, vegan

1 large sweet potato, peeled and thinly sliced

2 large russet potatoes, peeled and thinly sliced

3 teaspoons yellow curry powder

2 teaspoons ground turmeric

1 teaspoon garlic powder

1 teaspoon ground black pepper

1 teaspoon salt

2 tablespoons olive oil

TOOLS:

Vacuum sealer

Sous vide machine

1. Set sous vide and water bath for 185 degrees Fahrenheit.

2. In a large mixing bowl, toss the slices of sweet potato and russet potato with the curry powder, turmeric, garlic powder, black pepper, salt, and oil.

3. Divide the slices and herbs evenly among 2 large vacuum seal bags and seal.

4. Cook in the water bath for 20 minutes.

5. Empty the pouches into a serving platter and serve.

Sous Vide Eggplant and Herbs

Parsley, onion, and a little oil provide aromatics to the eggplant while it slowly cooks in a water bath. Many Wakandans eat a predominantly vegetarian diet and so we eat the eggplant because it is hearty and filling. You can quickly sear the sous vide eggplant in a pan with a little oil or cover and grill and serve with rice and a sauce like kale pesto or warmed msuzi matimati.

DIFFICULTY: Easy • **PREP TIME:** 10 minutes • **COOK TIME:** 45 minutes
YIELD: 4 to 6 servings • **DIETARY NOTES:** Gluten-free, vegan

1 large eggplant, sliced into ¼-inch rounds

3 tablespoons kosher salt

1 small yellow onion, halved and thinly sliced

6 sprigs fresh parsley

2 garlic cloves, crushed

1 teaspoon ground black pepper

3 tablespoons peanut oil

1 small bird's eye chile (optional)

2 tablespoons crushed roasted peanuts

TOOLS:

Vacuum sealer

Sous vide machine

1. Set sous vide and water bath for 185 degrees Fahrenheit.

2. In a large mixing bowl, toss the slices of eggplant with the salt to coat each one. Let sit for 20 minutes to release water.

3. Add onion slices, parsley, garlic, black pepper, peanut oil, and chile and toss.

4. Divide the eggplant slices and herbs evenly among 2 large vacuum seal bags and seal.

5. Cook in the water bath for 45 minutes.

6. To serve immediately, empty the pouches into a bowl.

7. You can serve them warm from the bag or, to add another texture, flash them over a hot grill to add some char.

8. Serve eggplant slices on a platter and garnish with the chopped peanuts.

9. Serve topped with warm Kale Pesto (page 26), Muhammara (page 19), or as a side with fish or meat and a side of rice.

10. The cooked eggplant can be chilled and stored in the bag for up to 4 days. Reheat by searing in a pan or by grilling on each side.

DRIED FRUITS AND RICE

When my grandparents were predominantly farming for the royal family, they often dried fruits that were in abundance and on the verge of turning. Mangoes, pineapple, and golden raisins are all dried fruits that would end up in a pot of rice seasoned with curry powder. The best result is when the bottom of the rice pot begins to crust and form a golden-brown color. Then the bottom is the most sought-after part of the rice.

DIFFICULTY: Advanced • **PREP TIME:** 35 minutes • **COOK TIME:** 50 minutes
YIELD: 6 servings • **DIETARY NOTES:** Gluten-free, nondairy, nut-free, vegan

2 cups basmati rice

1 tablespoon ground turmeric

1 teaspoon salt

½ cup mixed dried fruits (mango, papaya, pineapple)

½ cup coconut oil

Water

1. In a fine mesh strainer, rinse the rice with water until the water runs clear. Transfer the rice to a large bowl, cover with water, and let the rice soak for 30 minutes.

2. Strain the rice.

3. In a medium stockpot, bring 3 cups of water, the turmeric, and salt to a boil and stir in the rice. Cook the rice until al dente, about 4 minutes, then strain and return to the bowl.

4. Mix the dried fruit with the rice.

5. In a large, nonstick stockpot, melt the coconut oil over medium heat.

6. Cover the bottom of the pot with a layer of the rice and dried fruit mixture and press down into the bottom of the pot.

7. Scoop the remaining rice into the pot.

8. Using the end of a wooden spoon or a chopstick, poke 6 holes in the rice to allow for condensation to rise.

9. Cover the pot tightly and cook the rice over low heat for about 45 minutes, or until a nice brown layer has formed on the bottom of the rice and the rice is fully cooked.

10. To serve, either place a platter over the top of the pot and invert so that the bottom is on top; or scoop the rice out onto a platter and then, using a spatula, gently remove the crusty bottom and serve on top of the rice.

ROASTED PLANTAINS

S'Yan was a huge fan of roasted plantains and Chef Eli would prepare this for him regularly. Plantains are known as the "cooking banana." By using green plantains and then slowly roasting them, they caramelize and become a little sweet.

DIFFICULTY: Easy • **PREP TIME:** 5 minutes • **COOK TIME:** 40 minutes
YIELD: 4 to 6 servings • **DIETARY NOTES:** Gluten-free, nondairy, nut-free, vegan

4 ripe plantains

2 tablespoons peanut oil

1 tablespoon brown sugar

1 teaspoon salt

1. Preheat the oven to 375 degrees Fahrenheit.

2. Cut off the ends of the plantains and peel off the skin.

3. Cut the plantains in half crosswise and then cut those pieces in half lengthwise.

4. In a medium-sized mixing bowl, toss the plantain pieces with the oil, sugar, and salt.

5. Place plantains on a parchment-lined baking sheet and bake until tender golden on the edges, about 40 minutes.

6. Serve on the side with braised meats or vegetables.

NSIMA

Saucy dishes like braised goat, chicken, or kale and tomatoes pair well with this porridge. Cassava is grown throughout Wakanda and some of it is ground to make flour. Nsima can also be made by substituting corn meal, another common grain found in Wakanda.

DIFFICULTY: Medium • **PREP TIME:** 5 minutes • **COOK TIME:** 20 minutes
YIELD: 4 to 6 servings • **DIETARY NOTES:** Gluten-free, nondairy, nut-free, vegan

2 cups cassava flour
(or fine-ground cornmeal)

1 tablespoon salt

1. In a large saucepan bring water to a boil.

2. Turn heat down to medium and slowly add ½ cup of the cassava flour stirring with a wooden spoon to avoid clumps.

3. Continue adding the remaining flour and stirring until it is fully incorporated.

4. Let the porridge simmer, stirring occasionally until it becomes thick and transparent, about 10 minutes.

5. The nsima is finished when the porridge is thick and smooth. Serve in a dish to accompany fish, vegetables, or meat.

LAVASH

This is the recipe for the lavash made by the well admired bakers Kylee and Ayla. These sisters remind me of my own mother and Anti Bahiya. They went into business together and have an artisan bakery at the city market. The bakery was one of Queen Nanali's favorites. When I am asked to cater parties, I like to set out dips like kale pesto, muhammara, and chinananzi salsa to go with this crispy bread. You may find if using all-purpose flour that you have to knead the dough for an extra couple of minutes to build more gluten.

DIFFICULTY: Easy • **PREP TIME:** 5 minutes • **COOK TIME:** 10 minutes
YIELD: 4 to 6 servings • **DIETARY NOTES:** Nondairy, nut-free, vegan

3 cups cold water

2½ teaspoons active dry yeast

4 cups bread flour (or all-purpose flour)

1¼ teaspoons salt

¼ teaspoon sugar

½ teaspoon olive oil

Kosher salt

1. Preheat the oven to 350 degrees Fahrenheit.

2. In a large mixing bowl, combine water and yeast.

3. Add flour, salt, sugar, and oil and mix until fully incorporated.

4. Knead the dough for 3 minutes.

5. Divide the dough into 4 smaller balls.

6. To test the dough, first cut off a small piece from one of the balls. Hold the dough between your thumbs and index fingers and spread apart. If the dough stretches and is translucent, it is ready to roll out. If not, knead the dough balls for 2 more minutes.

7. Using a rolling pin, begin to roll out the balls into long rectangles. To keep the dough even, rotate it after each time you roll it. You want to roll them out as thinly as possible.

8. Gently place the rolled-out dough onto a greased baking sheet and bake until golden brown, about 10 minutes. Rotate the tray halfway through baking.

9. Remove from the oven and sprinkle with a pinch of kosher salt.

10. Break the bread into pieces and serve with dips or salsas.

MAIN
DISHES

VILLAGE-STYLE CURRIED CHICKEN

This dish is commonly made during tribal council meetings. Because it is best served after braising for many hours, the chefs start the stew before the meeting begins so that it will be ready to be served at the end. It has become a traditional dish in households across Wakanda and was the first item my mother and Anti Bahiya sold at the Birnin Zana Market. The bone marrow is a delicacy and usually saved for last.

DIFFICULTY: Medium • **PREP TIME:** 30 minutes • **COOK TIME:** 3 hours
YIELD: 6 servings • **DIETARY NOTES:** Gluten-free, nondairy, nut-free

1 tablespoon olive oil

1 large yellow onion, sliced ¼ inch thick

4 celery stalks, sliced into ¼-inch-thick half-moons

5 garlic cloves, chopped

3 carrots, cut into ¼-inch rounds

One 12-ounce can tomato paste

One 16-ounce can whole peeled tomatoes

½ cup yellow curry powder

1 whole chicken, cut into pieces

¼ cup lemon juice

Salt and pepper

1. In a large stockpot, heat oil over medium heat. Add onion and celery. Cook until translucent, about 2 minutes.

2. Add garlic and carrots. Cook while stirring occasionally for 2 minutes.

3. Add tomato paste and coat the vegetables.

4. Pour in whole peeled tomatoes and curry powder.

5. Add chicken. Cover ingredients with water until almost to the top of the pan. Bring to a boil and then lower heat.

6. Simmer for at minimum 3 hours until the meat has fallen off the bones. Finish by stirring in the lemon juice.

7. Salt and pepper to taste.

8. Serve the stew alongside Nsima (page 96) or rice. The bones are kept in the broth, and the marrow is generally saved for last as a delicacy.

ROASTED LAKE TROUT

My predecessor, Chef Eli, had the opportunity to cook for Captain America on his visits to Wakanda. This dish she prepared for a formal dinner at the Royal Palace, and afterwards, Captain America would request that Chef Eli make this dish at least once each time he was in the country. The recipe has since been a staple in the Royal Palace's recipe book.

DIFFICULTY: Easy • **PREP TIME:** 10 minutes • **COOK TIME:** 20 minutes
YIELD: 6 servings • **DIETARY NOTES:** Gluten-free, nondairy

2 tablespoons peanut oil

1 pound trout fillet (skin on)

1 lemon, sliced into 6 rounds

¼ cup Mango Ginger Sauce (page 21)

Salt and pepper

1. Preheat the oven to 350 degrees Fahrenheit.

2. Line a baking tray with foil.

3. Drizzle 1 tablespoon of peanut oil onto the tray. Place fillet skin down onto oiled foil.

4. Drizzle 1 tablespoon of peanut oil on top of the fillet.

5. Line the fillet with lemon slices and bake for 15 minutes.

6. After 15 minutes, remove the tray from the oven and pour the Mango Ginger Sauce on top.

7. Turn the oven up to a high broil and bake for another 5 minutes, or until the edges of the fillet have begun to brown.

8. Salt and pepper to taste.

9. Serve immediately.

Sweet and Spicy Oxtail with Cassava Dumplings

Often the Dora Milaje recommends restaurants in other countries for my apprentice, Mercy, and me to try while traveling. This recipe is inspired by a trip to the Caribbean. In Wakanda, we grow lots of cassava, and so I have incorporated the cassava flour dumpling with this sweet and spicy oxtail braise.

DIFFICULTY: Medium • **PREP TIME:** 20 minutes • **COOK TIME:** 3 to 4 minutes
YIELD: 2 to 3 servings • **DIETARY NOTES:** Gluten-free, nondairy

1 pound oxtail pieces (or beef shanks)

1 tablespoon vegetable oil

2 small yellow onions, sliced

2 bell peppers, medium diced

6 garlic cloves, minced

2 bird's eye chiles (or 1 small serrano pepper)

1 tablespoon tomato paste

5 fresh curry leaves

2 teaspoons ground turmeric

2 sprigs fresh oregano

3 cups vegetable stock

1 cup mango juice

Salt and pepper

DUMPLINGS

1 cup cassava flour (or tapioca flour, see note)

1 tablespoon cornmeal

½ teaspoon salt

¾ cup water

TO PREPARE THE OXTAIL:

1. Sprinkle the oxtail with salt and pepper.

2. Heat the oil in a medium braising pot over medium-high heat and add the oxtail pieces. Cook, about 1 minute per side, turning until each side is brown. Remove from the pot and set aside.

3. In the hot oil, sauté the onions, bell peppers, garlic, and chiles until they are caramelized, about 10 minutes.

4. Mix in the tomato paste, curry leaves, turmeric, and oregano.

5. Add the oxtail back into the pot and pour the vegetable stock and mango juice over it.

6. Cover pot and simmer on low for at least 3 hours. Leave it on longer for more tender meat.

7. Before serving, add the cassava dumplings and simmer for another 20 minutes.

TO MAKE THE DUMPLINGS:

8. In a medium mixing bowl, combine all ingredients and knead by hand until a smooth dough is formed. Depending on the type of flour and humidity in the room, you may need to add more water.

9. On a cutting board, roll the dough into a ball and cut into quarters.

10. Using the palms of your hands, roll each chunk of dough into a long snake. Cut each snake into ½-inch pieces.

11. Add to oxtail stew 20 minutes before serving.

 NOTE: If using tapioca flour, be aware that it has more starch and will make a denser dumpling than the cassava flour.

CASSAVA RAVIOLI

While eating around New York City, I fell in love with the pasta restaurants. I wanted to come up with a pasta that featured the native foods of Wakanda. The filling is a take on a traditional ravioli filling but highlights roasted cassava root and carrots. We don't use a lot of dairy, but there are some farmers in the villages outside of the Golden City that use their goat's milk to make cheese. I like to warm the kale pesto before tossing it with the ravioli.

DIFFICULTY: Advanced • **PREP TIME:** 45 minutes • **COOK TIME:** 20 minutes
YIELD: 4 to 6 servings • **DIETARY NOTES:** Nut-free

DOUGH

3 eggs

1 tablespoon olive oil

1 teaspoon salt

2 cups all-purpose flour

FILLING

2 large carrots, peeled and cut into thirds

3 large cassava root pieces, peeled and cored

1 tablespoon olive oil

2 tablespoons unsalted butter, melted

1 egg yolk

5 ounces fresh goat cheese

1 cup Kale Pesto (page 26)

Salt and pepper

TOOLS:

Food processor

Pasta roller

Ravioli cutter

TO MAKE THE DOUGH:

1. In a small bowl, whisk the eggs, olive oil, and salt.

2. In a larger bowl, form the flour into a pyramid with a hole in the middle.

3. Pour the eggs into the middle of the flour.

4. Using your hands, incorporate the flour into the eggs to make a dough.

5. Knead the dough until smooth, about 5 minutes.

6. Wrap the dough with plastic wrap and let it rest for 30 minutes.

TO PREPARE THE FILLING:

7. Preheat the oven to 400 degrees Fahrenheit.

8. In a medium bowl, toss the carrots and cassava with the oil. Salt and pepper to taste.

9. Lay the carrots and cassava out on a foil-lined baking tray and cover with foil. Bake until tender, about 30 minutes.

10. In the food processor, combine the cooked carrots, cassava, melted butter, and egg yolk.

11. Transfer the vegetable purée to a large bowl and mix in the goat cheese.

12. Salt and pepper to taste.

Continued on next page

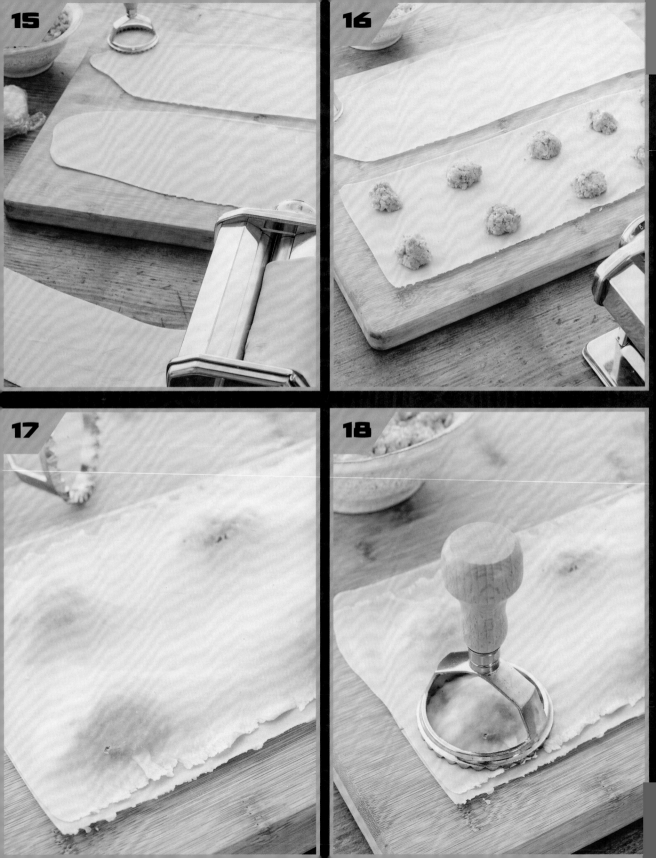

TO FORM THE RAVIOLI:

13. Cut the dough into 4 equal pieces.

14. Working with 1 piece at a time, flatten the dough with your palm into an oval.

15. Using a pasta roller or rolling pin, roll the dough out until it is thin enough to see your handprint through. Repeat with the rest of the dough.

16. Lay 2 sheets of dough out. On the 1st sheet, use a small spoon to portion out the filling into 2 rows with 5 spoonfuls in each row. Each spoonful should be about 1 ounce. Repeat on the 2nd sheet of dough.

17. Take the remaining sheets and place on top of the mounds of filling. Gently press out any air around the filling and press to seal.

18. Use the ravioli cutter to cut out shapes. Transfer cut pasta onto a floured baking tray.

19. Fill a large pot with water and bring to a boil.

20. Cook the ravioli in the water in 3-minute batches.

21. Using a slotted spoon, transfer the cooked pasta to a large bowl.

22. Toss the ravioli with the Kale Pesto and serve.

BRAISED LAMB STEW

Slow-braising meats is a tradition in Wakanda during times of conflict. It is to show the family is thinking of the conflict and supporting those who are fighting. You never know who will show up during these conflicts, needing a warm meal. When the tribal war occurred under T'Challa, I would often keep a pot of stew on the stove at all times. I like to use goat meat because it is fatty and even when braised for long times, the meat stays tender and moist. When goat is not readily available, lamb makes a good substitute.

DIFFICULTY: Advanced • **PREP TIME:** 15 minutes • **COOK TIME:** 3 hours
YIELD: 4 to 6 servings • **DIETARY NOTES:** Gluten-free, nondairy, nut-free

2 tablespoons olive oil

1 pound lamb stew meat

1 small yellow onion, sliced

3 medium carrots, sliced into rounds

2 celery stalks, sliced into half-moons

3 small Yukon potatoes, medium diced

4 garlic cloves, minced

1 bay leaf

1 cinnamon stick

1½ teaspoons ras el hanout

1½ teaspoons allspice

1 teaspoon ground ginger

1 lemon, juiced

2 tablespoons tomato paste

One 28-ounce can whole peeled tomatoes

2 cups beef broth

Salt

TOOLS:

Dutch oven

1. In a large Dutch oven, heat the olive oil over medium heat.

2. Salt the lamb pieces and add them to the oil. Brown the lamb pieces on each side, about 4 minutes per side.

3. Transfer the lamb to a paper towel–lined plate to drain.

4. Add the onion to the Dutch oven. Sauté for 2 minutes.

5. Add the carrots, celery, potatoes, and garlic. Sauté for another 2 minutes.

6. Stir in the bay leaf, cinnamon, ras el hanout, allspice, ginger, and lemon juice.

7. Add the lamb and tomato paste and stir until the vegetables are coated with the tomato paste.

8. Stir in the tomatoes and beef broth.

9. Cover and simmer on low heat for 3 hours, or until the lamb meat is tender.

10. Remove bay leaf and serve with a side of rice or Nsima (page 96).

SAVORY PLANTAIN CUSTARD

Whenever I am asked by King T'Challa to cater a dinner at the Wakandan Embassy I usually serve a number of small courses. This is one of my favorite dishes to serve. It is inspired by my travels to Asia where savory egg custards are often found. I smoke the plantains for a short time and then add them to the custard base before steaming. It can be served garnished with fresh diced mango and my favorite, braised goat.

DIFFICULTY: Easy • **PREP TIME:** 25 minutes • **COOK TIME:** 20 minutes
YIELD: 4 to 6 servings • **DIETARY NOTES:** Gluten-free, nut-free

2 ripe plantains

¼ cup vegetable oil

4 eggs

½ cup mango juice

½ cup vegetable broth

1 lime, juiced

1 tablespoon rice wine vinegar

1 tablespoon soy sauce

4 teaspoons Mango Gel (page 35)

TOOLS:

Blender

8 ounce ramekins

Sieve

1. Preheat the oven to 325 degrees Fahrenheit.

2. Peel the plantains and cut into ¼-inch rounds.

3. Heat the oil in a shallow sauté pan over medium-high heat.

4. Cook the plantains in the hot oil, about 2 minutes on each side, using a spatula or slotted spoon to flip them.

5. Drain on a paper towel–lined plate.

6. In the blender, combine the eggs, mango juice, vegetable broth, lime juice, rice wine vinegar, and soy sauce, and blend on high for 3 minutes.

7. Strain the egg mixture through a sieve and into a pitcher.

8. Place 2 slices of plantains into the ramekins.

9. Divide the egg mixture between the ramekins, pouring over the plantains and filling them half full.

10. Place the ramekins in an 8-by-12-inch baking pan.

11. Pour water into the baking pan to cover the bottom half of the ramekins.

12. Place the pan in the oven.

13. Bake until the custards are firm and jiggly, about 25 minutes.

14. Remove from the water and garnish each custard with a teaspoon of Mango Gel.

15. Custards can be served hot or cold.

BLACKENED TILAPIA

When I would travel to New York City to cook at the Wakandan Embassy, I would bring with me my apprentice, Mercy. Together we would tour the city trying out new foods. On one of our visits, we discovered this preparation for our nation's fish, chambo. I like this blackening technique because it gives a great char flavor without using fossil fuels.

DIFFICULTY: Medium • **PREP TIME:** 5 minutes
YIELD: 4 servings • **DIETARY NOTES:** Gluten-free, nondairy, nut-free

2 tablespoons onion powder

2 tablespoons garlic powder

2 tablespoons dried oregano

2 tablespoons light brown sugar

1 teaspoon salt

2 tablespoons paprika

1 tablespoon ground black pepper

4 tilapia fillets, thawed

TOOLS:

Cast-iron skillet

1. Heat the cast-iron skillet on high.

2. Mix onion powder, garlic powder, oregano, brown sugar, salt, paprika, and pepper together in a medium-sized bowl.

3. One at a time, coat each tilapia fillet by tossing in the mixing bowl.

4. Place fillets in hot skillet. Let one side develop a black or scorched crust and then flip. It is important to watch the fish. Depending on the skillet, it can take about 2 minutes to blacken. Fish are finished when each side is blackened.

STUFFED PUMPKIN WITH DRIED FRUITS AND RICE

In Wakanda, pumpkin is a universal term for all gourds and squashes. I like to use acorn, kabocha, or butternut squash because, when roasted, the flesh is caramelized and soft. When I fill the halves with the rice, it makes for a complete dish. I love this dish because it can be served family style or individually plated for a more formal dinner. The mango ginger sauce can either be drizzled over the top of the squash, or, if you are plating it individually, it can be dolloped on the plate first to provide a place for the squash to rest.

DIFFICULTY: Easy • **PREP TIME:** 5 minutes • **COOK TIME:** 45 minutes
YIELD: 2 to 4 servings • **DIETARY NOTES:** Gluten-free, nondairy, nut-free, vegan

1 medium squash (acorn, kabocha, butternut)

2 tablespoons olive oil

¼ cup orange juice

2 cups Dried Fruits and Rice (page 95)

1 cup Mango Ginger Sauce (page 21)

Salt and pepper

1. Preheat the oven to 350 degrees Fahrenheit.

2. Cut the squash lengthwise.

3. Drizzle the olive oil on the front and back of the squash.

4. Salt and pepper to taste.

5. Place the squash halves flesh side down on a foil- or parchment-lined baking tray.

6. Bake until soft, about 35 minutes.

7. Heat the orange juice in a sauté pan over medium heat and add the rice. Cook until warm, about 3 minutes.

8. To serve, scoop out the seeds from the cooked squash.

9. Divide the rice between the two halves, scooping the filling into the spot where the seeds were.

10. Drizzle the Mango Ginger Sauce on top of the rice and squash.

Desserts

MANGO SORBET WITH GINGER GRANITA

King T'Challa is a fan of frozen fruit sorbets. A granita is another frozen treat that can be shaved to enjoy on its own or to go on top of sorbet. We grow lots of ginger in Wakanda which is why I like to make a ginger-flavored granita to be a garnish for the frozen sorbets.

DIFFICULTY: Easy • **PREP TIME:** 10 minutes
YIELD: 6 servings • **DIETARY NOTES:** Gluten-free, nondairy, nut-free, vegan

3 cups cane sugar

2 cups water

1 lime, zested and juiced

1 cup mango purée

2 sprigs fresh mint

Ginger Granita (page 35) for garnishing

TOOLS:

Ice cream maker

1. In a medium saucepan, combine sugar and water and bring to a boil until sugar dissolves, about 2 minutes.

2. Turn off heat and add lime zest and juice and mango purée.

3. Transfer to a container and refrigerate until completely cooled down.

4. Following instructions on your ice cream maker, churn the sorbet base until it is frozen and smooth, about 45 minutes.

5. Transfer to a freezer-safe container and store frozen for up to two weeks.

6. Serve topped with fresh mint and Ginger Granita.

PAWPAW SORBET WITH GINGER GRANITA

Sorbets became popular in Wakanda shortly after T'Challa's return from studying at Oxford. On cold, rainy days he enjoyed stopping by a small bakery and ordering a cold treat to remind himself of home. He desired the dessert that he had become accustomed to treating himself to as a student and so he brought Chef Eli with him to Oxford to visit the restaurants run there by people who descended from Africa. They ate many different flavors of sorbets. When they returned Chef began experimenting with using liquid nitrogen to quickly freeze a syrup to serve one person or forty. We still use the liquid nitrogen technique in Wakanda, but I have modified this recipe to use a traditional ice cream churner/maker.

DIFFICULTY: Easy • **PREP TIME:** 10 minutes
YIELD: 6 servings • **DIETARY NOTES:** Gluten-free, nondairy, nut-free, vegan

3 cups cane sugar

2 cups water

1 lime, zested and juiced

1 puréed papaya

2 sprigs fresh mint

Ginger Granita (page 35) for garnishing

TOOLS:

Ice cream maker

1. In a medium saucepan, combine sugar and water and bring to a boil until sugar dissolves, about 2 minutes.

2. Turn off heat and add lime zest and juice and papaya purée.

3. Transfer to a container and refrigerate until completely cooled down.

4. Following instructions on your ice cream maker, churn the sorbet base until it is frozen and smooth, about 45 minutes.

5. Transfer to a freezer-safe container and store frozen for up to 2 weeks.

6. Serve topped with fresh mint and Ginger Granita.

Microwaved Banana and Walnut Cake

This is a classic childhood dessert for Wakandans. When you come home with your friends after school, you can just quickly whip up a couple of these cakes by going out and picking a few bananas and whisking the rest of the ingredients. While the royal kitchen boasts high-tech ovens that cook this almost instantly, if you don't have access to Wakandan tech, a commonplace microwave will also work for this recipe.

DIFFICULTY: Easy • **PREP TIME:** 5 minutes • **COOK TIME:** 2 minutes
YIELD: 1 serving • **DIETARY NOTES:** N/A

1 egg

1 teaspoon pure vanilla extract

2 tablespoons sugar

1 ripe banana

¼ cup whole milk

2 tablespoons unsalted butter, melted

½ cup all-purpose flour

1 tablespoon chopped toasted walnuts

½ teaspoon baking powder

¼ teaspoon salt

TOOLS:

Microwaveable cup

Microwave

1. Combine the egg and vanilla in a small mixing bowl and whisk together.

2. Add sugar, banana, milk, and butter and whisk until fully incorporated.

3. In a separate small bowl, combine flour, walnuts, baking powder, and salt.

4. Combine the banana mixture with the dry ingredients and pour into the microwaveable cup.

5. Microwave on high for 45 to 60 seconds and serve immediately.

DOUGHNUTS AND FOAMED COCOA

Deep frying is a cooking technique that is found across the continent of Africa. These pastries can be made with wheat flour or cassava flour. Some folks prefer to eat them plain. But I like to dust them with some cinnamon and sugar and serve them with a cup of warm milk and cocoa. This is a dish that would often be served at the open markets during the damp rainy season.

DIFFICULTY: Medium ● **PREP TIME:** 5 minutes ● **REST TIME:** 1 hour
COOK TIME: 5 minutes ● **YIELD:** 2 servings ● **DIETARY NOTES:** Nut-free

DOUGHNUTS

1 teaspoon active dry yeast

1 teaspoon granulated cane sugar plus more for dusting

2 tablespoons warm water

1 tablespoon unsalted butter

½ cup whole milk

1 egg

1½ cups all-purpose flour plus a pinch for dusting

1 teaspoon salt

2 cups vegetable oil

FOAMED COCOA

1 cup sweetened condensed milk

1 teaspoon pure vanilla extract

½ cup cocoa powder

2 cups whole milk

TOOLS:

Duch oven

Electric handheld milk frother

TO MAKE THE DOUGHNUTS:

1. Combine the yeast, sugar, and warm water together in a medium bowl and let rest for 20 minutes.

2. Heat the butter and milk in a small sauté pan over medium heat until the butter is melted. Set aside to cool.

3. Whisk the egg and cooled milk mixture into the yeast mixture.

4. Add the flour and salt and mix well.

5. Cover the dough with a damp towel and let rise in a warm place for 1 hour.

6. Punch the dough down and use your hands to knead the dough for 1 minute.

7. On a lightly floured cutting board, roll the dough into a long snake and cut into 2-inch pieces.

8. Roll the pieces into balls and place on a tray and let them rest for 10 minutes.

9. Heat the oil in a Dutch oven to 350 degrees Fahrenheit.

10. Fry the balls until light brown, about 45 seconds to 1 minute. Drain on a paper towel.

11. Toss the doughnuts in the sugar while still hot.

12. Serve on the side with warm foamed cocoa.

TO MAKE THE FOAMED COCOA:

13. In a medium saucepan, combine the condensed milk, vanilla, and cocoa powder. Warm over medium heat.

14. Slowly whisk in the milk until the cocoa powder is fully incorporated.

15. Remove the hot cocoa from heat.

16. Pour half of the cocoa into mugs.

17. With the reserved cocoa, use the electric frother to create a foam. Use a spoon to dollop each drink with the foam.

Whipped Sweet Potato and Candied Cinnamon

When I was a little girl, my mother would mash boiled sweet potatoes in a bowl and top it with cinnamon. It was a common snack for me while I was with her at the Birnin Zana Market. When I serve these for guests, I bake the sweet potatoes with cinnamon and sugar to create a sweet crust on top.

DIFFICULTY: Easy • **PREP TIME:** 20 minutes • **COOK TIME:** 5 minutes
YIELD: 6 servings • **DIETARY NOTES:** Nut-free

DOUGH

1¼ cups all-purpose flour

¼ teaspoon salt

½ cup cold unsalted butter, small diced

¼ cup cold water

SWEET POTATO

1 large sweet potato

2 eggs

½ cup unsalted butter, melted

1 tablespoon pure vanilla extract

1 cup brown sugar

½ cup whole milk

TOPPING

1 tablespoon ground cinnamon

1 tablespoon granulated cane sugar

TOOLS:

Six 8-ounce ramekins

Food processor

TO MAKE THE DOUGH:

1. Place the flour in a food processor with salt.

2. Turn on medium and gradually add the butter so that it crumbles in the flour.

3. Slowly add the water so that it incorporates into the dough.

4. Transfer to a flat surface and roll into a ball. Refrigerate for at least 20 minutes.

TO PREPARE THE SWEET POTATO:

5. Preheat the oven to 350 degrees Fahrenheit.

6. Poke holes in the sweet potato and bake until tender, about 35 to 45 minutes.

7. Once cooled, peel the sweet potato and place in the food processor.

8. While on medium-high speed, mix into the sweet potato the eggs, butter, vanilla, and brown sugar until fully incorporated.

9. Slowly add the milk. Turn on high for 45 seconds.

TO SERVE:

10. Roll out dough using a rolling pin until it is ¼-inch thick. Use the ramekins as molds to cut out 6 rounds.

11. Press the rounds into the bottom of the ramekins.

12. Divide the sweet potato mixture evenly between the ramekins.

13. Place them on a baking sheet and bake for 15 minutes.

14. Mix the cinnamon and sugar together and sprinkle a thin layer across the top of the sweet potatoes.

15. Bake for another 15 minutes. Serve immediately.

BASBOUSA

Basbousa is traditionally known to be a dense and creamy cake. I have seen it all over the world. In this recipe, you can use either cassava flour or semolina. The sisters who run the bakery in the Birnin Azzaria market, Kylee and Ayla, would make this cake and serve squares of it in their store. On special occasions, such as the birth of a child or a wedding, I like to serve this dessert. I have tested it with the semolina flour and with our native cassava flour and have gotten the same rich cake results.

DIFFICULTY: Easy • **PREP TIME:** 10 minutes • **COOK TIME:** 30 minutes
YIELD: 6 servings • **DIETARY NOTES:** Gluten-free

CAKE

1 tablespoon pan spray

1 cup sugar

2 eggs

¼ cup whole milk

1 cup heavy cream

½ teaspoon vanilla extract

1¾ cups cassava or fine semolina flour

½ cup dried unsweetened coconut flakes

1 teaspoon baking powder

8 tablespoons unsalted butter, melted

SYRUP

½ cup water

1 cup granulated cane sugar

½ tablespoon rose water (or orange blossom water)

½ lemon, juiced

⅔ cup pistachios, chopped

TO MAKE THE CAKE:

1. Preheat the oven to 350 degrees Fahrenheit.

2. With the pan spray, grease an 8-by-10-inch baking pan.

3. In a large mixing bowl, whisk the sugar, eggs, milk, cream, and vanilla.

4. In a separate large bowl, mix the cassava flour, coconut, and baking powder.

5. Combine the egg mixture, melted butter, and flour until evenly incorporated.

6. Pour batter into the baking pan and bake for 30 minutes, or until the cake is golden brown on top.

TO PREPARE THE SYRUP:

7. In a small saucepan, bring the water and sugar to a boil and simmer until the sugar dissolves, about 2 minutes.

8. Remove from the heat and whisk in the rose water and lemon juice.

FOR ASSEMBLY:

9. Pour the syrup over the baked cake and sprinkle chopped pistachios evenly on top.

DRINKS

GINGER TONIC

This recipe is one I learned while working at the Royal Palace. The beverage director, Ms. Loyiso, had been there since the time of King Azzuri and explained to me that the king insisted on having a ginger tonic with his dinners. And so, she came up with this recipe for making and bottling this elixir. You do have to have some patience, but in the end, you'll have a delicious beverage!

DIFFICULTY: Advanced • **PREP TIME:** 15 minutes • **FERMENTATION TIME:** 12 days
YIELD: 10 servings • **DIETARY NOTES:** Gluten-free, nondairy, nut-free, vegan

18 cups water

1 cup lemon juice

2 cups minced fresh ginger

1 teaspoon active dry yeast

3 cups sugar

TOOLS:

Clip top bottles

1. In a medium-sized, airtight container combine 2 cups of water, ½ cup of lemon juice, ginger, yeast, and 1 cup of sugar. Refrigerate and let the ginger brine in the yeast mixture for 5 days.

2. In a large stock pan, boil 2 cups of sugar with 4 cups of water until the sugar is dissolved, about 4 minutes, and let it cool down.

3. Combine the ginger base and sugar syrup with 12 cups of water and mix well.

4. Strain the ginger and bottle the liquid. Store refrigerated and wait for at least 5 days before drinking.

GINGER TURMERIC LEMONADE

It gets very hot in sub-Saharan Africa, so having a place to stop off for a cool drink while traveling is always appreciated. Lemonade stands are very common throughout Wakanda. In the markets of Birnin Djata and Birnin S'Yan, and at drink stands along the major roadways that lead to the Golden City, this is a popular drink.

DIFFICULTY: Easy • **PREP TIME:** 10 minutes • **YIELD:** 1 serving
DIETARY NOTES: Gluten-free, nondairy, nut-free, vegan

¼ cup cane sugar

½ cup water

3 lemons, peeled and quartered

One 2-inch piece fresh ginger, peeled

Two 1-inch pieces fresh turmeric, peeled

Ice for serving

TOOLS:

Juicer

1. In a small saucepan, combine sugar and water over medium-high heat. Simmer until the sugar is dissolved, about 2 minutes, and then remove from heat.

2. Following the specific juicer instructions, press the lemon, ginger, and turmeric into a container.

3. Mix the sugar syrup in with the pressed juices. Pour in a glass over ice.

BISSAP SPRITZ

This is a natural soda using a homemade simple syrup flavored with hibiscus. You can use a home water carbonator or canned soda water and, depending on how sweet you want it, you can add more hibiscus syrup. Bissap spritz can be found in markets throughout Wakanda. Wakandans are used to pure cane sugar sweeteners, utilizing their natural resources rather than creating cheaper, less healthy alternatives. This recipe uses a syrup made with pure cane sugar.

DIFFICULTY: Easy • **PREP TIME:** 5 minutes • **COOK TIME:** 3 minutes
YIELD: 12 ounces of syrup • **DIETARY NOTES:** Gluten-free, nondairy

HIBISCUS SYRUP

2 cups cane sugar

2 cups water

2 cups hibiscus flowers

SPRITZ (PER SERVING)

1 lime, juiced

¼ cup Hibiscus Syrup

1 cup carbonated water (or club soda)

1 sprig fresh mint

Ice for serving

TOOLS:

Water carbonator

TO MAKE THE HIBISCUS SYRUP:

1. In a small saucepan, bring cane sugar, water, and hibiscus to a boil until the sugar dissolves, about 2 minutes. Turn off heat and let the flowers steep in the liquid for an hour.

2. Strain the flowers. The syrup can be stored refrigerated for 1 week.

TO PREPARE THE SPRITZ:

3. In a glass, mix lime juice and Hibiscus Syrup.

4. Fill the glass with ice and top with carbonated water.

5. Garnish with the sprig of mint.

Coconut Mango Smoothie

This is a popular cool treat enjoyed by young and older Wakandans. The key is to use frozen mango and pineapple; that way no ice needs to be added. The coconut milk and banana create a creamy and frothy beverage. When she was younger, Princess Shuri often asked Ms. Loyiso for a round for her and her friends after a day of playing and swimming.

DIFFICULTY: Easy • **PREP TIME:** 10 minutes • **YIELD:** 10 servings
DIETARY NOTES: Gluten-free, nondairy, nut-free, vegan

1½ cups frozen mango chunks

1½ cups frozen pineapple chunks

1 banana

1 cup coconut milk

1 cup fresh orange juice

1 teaspoon cane sugar

1½ teaspoons ground cinnamon

TOOLS:

Blender

1. In a blender, combine mango, pineapple, banana, coconut milk, orange juice, sugar, and 1 teaspoon of cinnamon. Blend until smooth, about 1 minute.

2. Pour the blended drink into glasses. Sprinkle the remaining cinnamon on top.

ORANGE CARROT JUICE

As Princess Shuri got older, she began to request more fresh-pressed juices in the morning. She loves to drink this juice in the morning because of the wake-up kick she gets from the fresh ginger. Sometimes I make a big batch and bottle the extra so that she can grab them when she needs. If the carrot or ginger is too strong for your tastes, you can cut the juice with a little carbonated water.

DIFFICULTY: Easy • **PREP TIME:** 10 minutes
YIELD: 1 serving • **DIETARY NOTES:** Gluten-free, nondairy, nut-free, vegan

2 navel oranges, peeled and quartered

3 medium carrots, peeled and quartered

1 lemon, peeled and quartered

One 1-inch piece fresh ginger, peeled

½ cup carbonated water (optional)

Ice for serving

TOOLS:

Juicer

1. Following the specific juicer instructions, press the oranges, carrots, lemon, and ginger into a container.

2. Mix with a spoon and pour into a glass over ice. If you'd like to add a little bubble, top with some carbonated water.

TAMARIND COLA

Many cola recipes require a brown syrup or coloring. This recipe uses tamarind as a natural flavoring and coloring. When young T'Challa and Shuri would have their special movie nights, a batch of this cola was made for them to accompany their snack of harissa popcorn.

DIFFICULTY: Medium • **PREP TIME:** 10 minutes • **COOK TIME:** 5 minutes
YIELD: 2 cups syrup • **DIETARY NOTES:** Gluten-free, nondairy, nut-free

2 whole cinnamon sticks

1 teaspoon coriander seed

1 tablespoon star anise

2 cups sugar

2 whole vanilla beans, split

2 cups water

2 large oranges, zested and juiced

1 lime, zested and juiced

1 lemon, zested and juiced

½ teaspoon freshly grated nutmeg

½ cup tamarind concentrate

Ice for serving

TOOLS:

Water carbonator/syphon

TO PREPARE THE SYRUP:

1. In a small sauté pan, toast the cinnamon, coriander, and anise over medium-high heat until aromatic, about 1 to 2 minutes.

2. Transfer to a small saucepan with the sugar, vanilla, water, orange zest, lime zest, and lemon zest. Bring to a boil and simmer until sugar is completely dissolved, about 2 minutes.

3. Remove from heat and whisk in orange juice, lime juice, lemon juice, nutmeg, and tamarind concentrate.

TO MAKE THE COLA:

4. Pour ½ cup of syrup into a tall glass.

5. Fill halfway with ice.

6. Pour 1½ cups of carbonated water and stir.

AVOCADO SMOOTHIE

The training center for the Dora Milaje has a fresh juice and smoothie bar for all the trainees. Avocado has such a rich and creamy texture that adding it to a smoothie makes a consistency similar to ice cream. At the training center, we use liquid nitrogen to freeze many of our cold beverages. This recipe calls for ice to give the extra, almost bitter coldness that the liquid nitrogen would provide.

DIFFICULTY: Easy • **PREP TIME:** 5 minutes • **YIELD:** 2 servings
DIETARY NOTES: Gluten-free, nondairy, nut-free

1 avocado, halved and peeled

1 banana, peeled and cut into chunks

½ cup frozen pineapple

1 cup baby spinach (or baby kale)

1 lime, zested and juiced

1 cup coconut milk

½ cup ice cubes

1 tablespoon grade A maple syrup

TOOLS:

Blender

1. Combine all ingredients into a blender on high until smooth.
2. Divide into two glasses and serve.

COCOA ICED COFFEE

Ms. Loyiso is the beverage director that I worked with at the Royal Palace. When Captain America began to visit Wakanda, she created this drink for his enjoyment. It uses the coffee beans that are native to Wakanda—that we roast and then freeze dry—sweetened with condensed milk and cocoa.

DIFFICULTY: Easy • **PREP TIME:** 5 minutes
YIELD: 1 serving • **DIETARY NOTES:** Gluten-free, nut-free

2 tablespoons instant coffee

1 tablespoon cocoa powder

3 tablespoons hot water

1 cup sweetened condensed milk

Ice for serving

1. In a tall glass, combine coffee, cocoa, and hot water. Stir until dissolved.

2. Fill the glass half full with ice.

3. Add the condensed milk and stir.

ORANGE SMASH

This drink is our version of the orange cream soda. We use the peel and juice from oranges to make a sugar syrup with fresh vanilla bean. Many Wakandans grow up drinking a sobo beverage mixing the fruit concentrate with water.

DIFFICULTY: Medium • **PREP TIME:** 10 minutes • **COOK TIME:** 5 minutes
YIELD: 2 cups syrup • **DIETARY NOTES:** Gluten-free, nondairy, nut-free

3 cups sugar

2 cups water

2 fresh vanilla bean pods or 1 teaspoon pure vanilla extract

3 large oranges, peeled and juiced

Ice for serving

TOOLS:

Water carbonator/syphon

TO PREPARE THE SYRUP:

1. Slice the vanilla bean pod in half lengthwise and use a knife to scrape out the inside of the pods into a small saucepan.

2. Add the sugar, water, and orange peels to the saucepan and combine. Bring to a boil. Simmer until the sugar is dissolved, about 2 minutes.

3. Remove from heat and let cool.

4. Strain the orange peels and stir in the orange juice. If you are using the vanilla extract instead of the beans, add it here.

5. Store refrigerated for up to 1 week.

TO MAKE THE SMASH:

6. Pour ½ cup of syrup into a tall glass.

7. Fill halfway with ice.

8. Pour 1½ cups of carbonated water and stir.

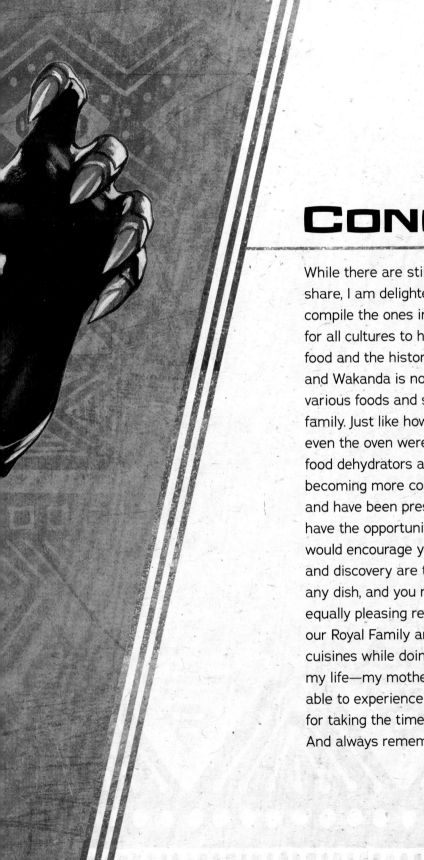

CONCLUSION

While there are still many more Wakandan recipes to share, I am delighted to have had the opportunity to compile the ones included here for you. It is important for all cultures to have written documentation of their food and the history that goes along with those dishes, and Wakanda is no different. I hope you enjoy trying the various foods and sharing them with your friends and family. Just like how the blender, food processor, and even the oven were once new culinary technologies, food dehydrators and home sous vide machines are becoming more commonplace in modern societies and have been present in Wakanda for years. If you have the opportunity to use such culinary devices, I would encourage you to do so. But if not, creativity and discovery are the most important ingredients in any dish, and you may find your own methods produce equally pleasing results. I have had the honor of serving our Royal Family and traveling the world, learning various cuisines while doing so. It is because of the women in my life—my mother, anti, and grandmother—that I was able to experience such a great opportunity. Thank you for taking the time to learn about our food and history. And always remember, Wakanda lives within us all.

ABOUT THE AUTHOR

Nyanyika Banda is a Malawian-American professional chef, writer, and scholar of the foodways of the African diaspora. Born in the United States, and raised between New England and the Midwest, Banda has always used food as a way to connect to her heritage. She has worked in some of the United States' top restaurants in New York, San Francisco, Los Angeles, and Atlanta and has traveled the world as a private chef. In 2018 she won an Eater Award for her pop-up turned brick-and-mortar restaurant.

After working in the restaurant industry for nearly twenty years, she returned to school to study history and writing. She designed her degree around the history of African foodways and has been an independent scholar ever since. Banda has contributed to Food52, Thrillist, Saveur, and RESY and has an essay in the book *Knives and Ink*.

Banda recalls cooking with her Malawian aunt, who was always eager to share the traditional foods of their family's village. Banda looked forward to holidays as a young chef, when her aunt would prepare braised meats and greens, smoked fish, and nsima.

The Wakanda Cookbook is a celebration of the food of the great continent of Africa, as imagined through the lens of the fictional nation of Wakanda.

Special Thanks

For my Auntie Rose, the original Chef of our clan. Thank you for bringing me home, finally, and for always bringing home to me.

— Nyanyika Banda

INSIGHT EDITIONS

PO Box 3088
San Rafael, CA 94912
www.insighteditions.com

[f] Find us on Facebook: www.facebook.com/InsightEditions
[t] Follow us on Twitter: @insighteditions

Library of Congress Cataloging-in-Publication Data available.

ISBN: 978-1-64722-359-5

Publisher: Raoul Goff
VP of Licensing and Partnerships: Vanessa Lopez
VP of Creative: Chrissy Kwasnik
VP of Manufacturing: Alix Nicholaeff
Editorial Director: Vicki Jaeger
Designer: Brooke McCullum
Senior Editor: Jennifer Sims
Associate Editor: Harrison Tunggal
Senior Production Editor: Elaine Ou
Production Manager: Sam Taylor
Production Associate: Deena Hashem
Senior Production Manager, Subsidiary Rights: Lina s Palma

Photographer: Ted Thomas
Food and Prop Stylist: Elena P. Craig
Assistant Food Stylist: August Craig

 ROOTS of PEACE   [tree] REPLANTED PAPER

Insight Editions, in association with Roots of Peace, will plant two trees for each tree used in the manufacturing of this book. Roots of Peace is an internationally renowned humanitarian organization dedicated to eradicating land mines worldwide and converting war-torn lands into productive farms and wildlife habitats. Roots of Peace will plant two million fruit and nut trees in Afghanistan and provide farmers there with the skills and support necessary for sustainable land use.

Manufactured in China by Insight Editions

10 9 8 7 6 5 4 3 2 1